AN ENERGETIC AND MINDFUL APPROACH
TO PREGNANCY AND MOTHERHOOD

Mel Braun

Magic Mama: An Energetic and Mindful Approach to Pregnancy and Motherhood
©Mel Braun

All rights reserved. This book or any portion thereof may not be reproduced or used in any manner whatsoever without the express written permission of the publisher except for the use of brief quotations in a book review.

ISBN: 979-8-35098-544-3 (soft cover)
ISBN: 979-835099-014-0 (hard cover)

Dedicated to my son, Roczen. Thank you for making me a mother. You're the gift in life I didn't know I needed. Without you, this book wouldn't be possible. You're not only a light in my life but will now be a light in the lives of many, as you also helped me birth this book and its beautiful message. I love you.

ACKNOWLEDGEMENTS

A special thank you to Amy JD Hillard for editing this book. We shared countless hours, laughs, and tears while working together, which deepened our friendship. This book wouldn't be what it is without you.

To LeeMarie Photography, I appreciate you capturing my sweet baby bump for the cover of this book. Your artistic talent is impressive, and I will cherish the photos you've taken forever.

TABLE OF CONTENTS

Introduction	1
Chapter 1. Follow the Crumbs	9
Chapter 2. Why Reiki	26
Chapter 3. Reiki and the Physical Body	42
Chapter 4. Your Energy Body	53
Chapter 5. Energetic Responsibility	67
Chapter 6. The Emotional Body	83
Chapter 7. Mindful Mama	100
Chapter 8. Preparing to Conceive	120
Chapter 9. The Butterfly Effect	135
Chapter 10. Good Vibe Tribe	148
Chapter 11. Baby Communication	162
Chapter 12. Mama's Intuition	177
Chapter 13. Birth	195
Chapter 14. The 4th Trimester	210
Chapter 15. Raising an Energetically Aware Child	226
Final Thoughts	236
Index	238

INTRODUCTION

Someone once compared me to a fairy, fluttering and sprinkling magical pixie dust on everything around me. Initially, I was uncertain how to interpret their remark. True to my polite ways, I smiled and nodded, responding in my gentle southern accent, "Awe, thanks so much."

Their comment lingered in my mind, making me question whether they were teasing me or being sincere. Upon deeper reflection, I understood their intent clearly. From their perspective, I lead a life reminiscent of a fairytale, swept off my feet by a charming prince, blessed with a wonderfully cheerful son who smiles endlessly, and overall, my life seems to veer towards the positive rather than the negative. However, what remains unseen is the inner journey and effort that have brought me to this stage in my life.

I was raised in a middle-class family in a neighborhood where I was the only girl on the street. Being an only child in that environment, I quickly learned to defend myself with a tough and outspoken demeanor, warning the neighbor's son that I would pull him off his dirt bike and beat him up if he harmed my dog. In middle school, I was the only girl on the eighth-grade football team, I played soccer, was in the school choir, and became interested in modeling and acting. Sadly, keeping busy with extracurriculars and the protective facade I had created only took me so far. I still experienced emotional scars that I kept hidden. This buried secret eventually surfaced in unexpected ways in my early twenties, but these scars didn't stop me from daydreaming about the life I wanted.

At 15, when I got my learner's permit, an upscale housing community was being built that I would drive past on my way to work. It was gated but remained accessible to construction workers during the day. I would drive through the neighborhood in my 1989 Plymouth Voyager van, which was rusted on top (we called it Carrot Top after the comedian), and it creaked when I would drive over speed bumps. It had no heat or air conditioning, but since my parents only paid $500 for it, what could I really expect?

Driving through this neighborhood, I fantasized about what it would be like to live in such elegant homes. One house featured a quaint vineyard in the side yard, while others displayed expansive circular driveways with magnificent fountains at their center. These mansions were truly storybook value, especially for a girl living in a mobile home.

Eventually, this became the neighborhood where Carolina Panthers players and NASCAR drivers lived. Once enough of the homes had been completed and occupied by these celebrities, the gate remained fully closed at all times. Clearly, no one was giving me or my rusty old van a code to get in.

I was too embarrassed to be seen driving my van to high school, so I drove to a friend's house, parked there, and rode with her to school in her red Ford Probe. Then, after school, I would ride with her back to her house, change into my work clothes, and drive to Concord Mills Mall to work at one of the many kiosks in the middle.

At one time, I sold magic tricks and pranks, using my juggling skills in the mall to attract customers. Later, I transitioned to selling cell phone accessories, where I truly thrived. Earning $5 an hour plus a 5% commission on my sales, I quickly made at least $1,200 monthly. This income helped me save enough to buy a white 1988 Honda Accord Coupe, which made me feel quite accomplished. It had heat and air conditioning and was much sportier than a van, though the sunroof leaked. Nonetheless, I was proud to have purchased it entirely on my own and could afford fuel, insurance, and my monthly cell phone bill.

Throughout high school, I worked around 25 hours each week. After graduating, I secured a job at Auto Bell car wash, still aspiring for the life I envisioned. During this time, I traveled to Hollywood and met with a prospective talent agent in hopes of realizing my dream of becoming an actress, but it wasn't in the cards.

One day at the car wash, a stylish young man pulled up in his sleek black Mercedes with shiny rims. Naturally, I seized the opportunity to upsell him on tire gloss to highlight those rims. He became a regular, and eventually, my 18-year-old self gathered the courage to ask him about his job. He told me he and his father had recently relocated from California and started their own real estate company focusing on property management.

During his next visit to the car wash, he approached me and inquired if I would like to become a leasing agent for his company. Unsure of what a leasing agent was or what the role entailed, I asked several questions. The following day, I attended the interview and was hired on the spot.

After renting single-family homes for a while, I found it difficult to manage the gas expenses for property showings along with my living expenses. Consequently, I applied for a leasing agent role at a nearby apartment community. With leasing experience now on my resume and a tenacious spirit, I was hired immediately. Although I was the youngest leasing team member, my dedication and professionalism consistently positioned me as the top producer. My determination propelled me rapidly up the corporate ladder.

At this apartment community, I met my now husband. During that time, my manager was married to my husband's truck chief from his rookie NASCAR year. They believed we would hit it off, but I had my doubts. I had heard enough rumors about how race car drivers treated women and didn't want to become just another story. My manager urged me to at least give it a chance since, as she put it, "He came with references." So, I agreed to just one date.

While sitting across from him at a table at The Melting Pot, we shared fondue, laughs, and conversation. It felt like reconnecting with an old friend after many years and then picking up where we had left off. It felt comfortable and familiar, even though we had just met. As I sat across from him, I thought to myself, "he is going to be my husband." He was just 19, and I was 21. We met on a Monday, became 'official' by Friday, and moved in together six weeks later.

As I progressed in my property management career in my early twenties, I began to feel significant burnout. Frequently, I was sent home early at the end of the week due to logging too much overtime. The onset of shingles was a major warning sign that I needed to make a change. My body was clearly under immense stress, even though my still-maturing mind did not fully comprehend the situation.

At that point, I chose to pursue a new path by obtaining my real estate license. The flexibility of creating my own schedule appeared less daunting and gave me a chance to attend some of my then-boyfriend's races. This decision came in 2009, shortly after the housing market crash. Many believed I was unwise to enter the field during such a downturn. After earning my Broker's license, I relied on my professional leasing background and joined a boutique real estate firm specializing in property management and sales. The property management aspect provided additional income in an area where I excelled while also allowing me to grasp the basics of sales and successfully close multiple deals each year.

As time passed, I established lasting relationships with my clients, leading my business to thrive through referrals. In my late twenties, as I came to own and operate my own real estate firm, I discovered a crucial aspect of myself: I was an empath. This meant I carried not only my stress and emotions but also those of my clients. While being an empath enhanced my ability to connect deeply with clients, it led to significant burnout again. Although the freedom to create my own schedule seemed less stressful at first, the absence of a steady paycheck compelled me to work far beyond the typical 9-5 hours. My work started to dominate my life. I found myself negotiating deals at midnight to meet expectations, particularly in a competitive market where timing was critical. Despite needing ample sleep, I struggled to rest as my mind always raced. It was during this time that my husband recommended I try meditation to help alleviate my stress.

After I made meditation a daily habit, I discovered my magic recipe. I began exploring energy and its impact on everyone, particularly empaths. My journey into meditation deepened alongside various spiritual and mindfulness practices. I started applying my newfound knowledge and soon saw remarkable benefits. I found myself feeling less stressed, even in challenging situations. This calmness contributed to improved sleep, and I felt more positive overall. I had truly transformed my life for the better.

I will always be thankful for Real Estate, as it was the foundation that directed me toward my true path. This journey led me to become a

Medical Reiki Master, a mindfulness educator, and a 200-hour Yoga Teacher Trainer, while also earning certifications in pre and postnatal yoga.

With now over a decade invested in my energetic healing journey, I realize the tears and challenges were the necessary discomfort I needed to experience to get me where I am today. Each triumph showed me how the Universe consistently introduced the right people at the perfect moments. With an open mind and heart, I blindly followed the trail of breadcrumbs laid out before me and trusted the process. This was especially true when I decided I was ready to become a mother.

Once I became pregnant, I realized I wasn't reinventing the wheel through this process. My body was designed to give birth. Yet, through this season of life, I noticed an essential element was missing. With my background and expertise in energy work and mindfulness, I was led to search past my physical body to connect deeper with my mental, emotional, and spiritual self for the prenatal care I needed. During this process, I realized the hardships I had endured through my energetic healing journey had unknowingly been training me for pregnancy and motherhood. My experiences inspired the creation of this book, aiming to support others through their journeys of pregnancy, childbirth, and motherhood.

The views and opinions expressed throughout this book are not designed to replace the advice of medical professionals but are to compliment them. As you read along, I encourage you to subscribe to an open mind and explore the innovative ideas and concepts presented. Some sections of this book may resonate with you instantly, while others might appear unusual or unconventional. It is not a coincidence you felt drawn to this book. I know messages are waiting for you among these pages.

Introduction

With this book becoming a staple on your bookshelf, you can access it throughout your pregnancy journey and beyond. As you refer to it at different stages, concepts that once seemed far-fetched will resonate and become plausible when the information is intended to align with you.

You will start to perceive and feel things on a different level. In motherhood, trusting your intuition and safeguarding your energy is essential. You will realize that you are far more than what meets the eye; you are matter, energy, and a soul. I will demonstrate the significance of deeply understanding this and its impact on every facet of your life. With a solid grasp of your energy body, you will fully access your personal power and innate wisdom.

Your mind can create your reality, especially during pregnancy, childbirth, and motherhood. I will guide you in harnessing the power of your mind and assist you in rewiring your thoughts so you can reach your goals. Beyond teaching mindfulness practices, I will provide scientific explanations to help you understand the core principles behind these techniques and their functions. With increased awareness and consistent effort, you can learn to control your mind rather than allowing it to control you.

The stories you will encounter throughout this book are bound to touch your heart, give you chills, and highlight the magic that surrounds you daily. If you've repeatedly encountered adversities in your life or during your journey to motherhood, this book will restore your faith and empower you to persevere.

Simply reading this book alone and understanding these topics will not be the driving force of your pregnancy, birth, and motherhood. You must embody the information given to optimize your experiences and outcomes. You will see you are the alchemist of your life.

From this moment forward, understand you are magic, mama. It's time to discover your inner divine and ignite your power. You possess the ability to create your future and foster a healthier one for your child or children. Together, we are cultivating conscious motherhood.

Before diving deeper into this book, I want to thank the woman who lovingly referred to me as a fairy. She had no idea that her words would motivate me to seek my true calling, aiding others through the insights I've acquired throughout my journey. These meaningful changes transformed my life, allowing me to create my own fairy tale, and you can do the same. As the clever fairy Tinkerbell from Peter Pan famously said, "All you need is faith, trust, and a little bit of pixie dust."

The names in this book have been changed to protect the identity of the individuals sharing their stories.

CHAPTER 1

Follow the Crumbs

I never felt I needed to become a mother to be complete. Being an only child and then wife to a frequent traveler, I had grown accustomed to and quite fond of my alone time. Our free-spirited lifestyle of impromptu date nights and traveling the world together suited us well for the first 15 years; until it didn't.

It was a typical July summer day, hot with stifling humidity, so I was inside cleaning the house. While dusting my desk in the office, I heard a little girl's voice say, "I'm ready when you are. The world needs me." I stopped and stared at the wall with a look of confusion, wondering who I was hearing or, honestly, if I was daydreaming. Then I heard her introduce herself as "Aria Sky."

I waited a few weeks before telling my husband what had happened, wondering what he'd think. Would he be open-minded about my communication with a spirit or believe I was officially off my rocker? Frankly, I was questioning my own psyche. Surprisingly, the conversation opened the door to us deciding we were ready to start a family. During this conversation, we decided to wait until the following year to begin trying in hopes the timing of my conceiving would line up with his travel schedule. Until the time was right, we continued our regular scheduled life.

It was just shy of fall, and Sedona's magic was summoning me. The connection I had felt previously with the red rocks, energy vortexes, our indigenous people, and its mysticism intrigued me. Little did I know there was nothing that could prepare me for the magic of this trip.

Once landing in Phoenix, my Reiki friend and I rented a car and drove two scenic hours to Sedona. As we reached the limits of Sedona, the bright glow of the red and orange rocks in the distance gave me full-body chills. I felt at home and elated to be back.

Our first day was action-packed. We hiked through Buddha Beach as we made our way to the butte of Cathedral Rock, had lunch mountainside, then hiked back to our Airbnb, concluding our six-mile round-trip hike. We quickly regrouped and headed to the meeting spot for our three-hour tour with our Shamanic Guide.

We began our tour at Enchantment Resort, where our guide led us through a meditation as he drummed and chanted Native American hems. The smell of the fresh mountain air, the melody of his voice, and each drum beat reverberated through my body and took me into a deep, meditative state. All my senses were heightened even though my mind was completely blank.

A low rumble of thunder in the distance intensified the beating of the drum and his chanting. It began to drizzle as he slowly brought us out of our hypnotic state. The rain felt like a gift from the heavens above, gently washing away the old to make room for the new. Our guide then pointed behind us; a perfect rainbow was framed between the rocks of the mountain. It stayed long enough for us all to capture a few photos on our phones and then disappear. The pure magic of nature chiming in at that moment showed we were all being supported by a higher force. The rain increased to a steady downfall. We loaded back into his SUV and headed to Rachel's Knoll.

Once arriving, my body and soul remembered the healing that had taken place at that very spot during my last visit. I had retrieved my power and reclaimed parts of myself that had been lost. The shifts from that experience left a lasting impression. Tears gently fell down my face as I realized I had become the woman I aspired to be, that I always knew was within me. I had reached pure contentment and happiness and was living my soul's mission. The gratitude I felt at that moment flooded my heart.

As our intimate group stood on the rock of Rachel's Knoll, we started to feel and see the shifts happening with the weather. In the distance, we watched the storm roll in over the mountains and observed in awe. We took pictures and videos on our phones of the lightning strikes in the distance. An attendee in the group caught a lightning strike at the right moment, capturing one of my all-time favorite photos. It is the perfect depiction of "where there is darkness, there is light."

Before leaving, we all stood in a circle and held hands as we listened to the acoustics of the storm play in the background. We each said a prayer aloud and followed it up with a chant to bless our prayers.

As we were venturing to our last destination, our guide pointed to a mountain we were passing called Mescal Mountain and specifically mentioned a section called the Birthing Cave. The indigenous Hopi women would go to this cave when giving birth as they found this sacred site spiritual and uplifting. When standing on the canyon floor and looking up, the outside of the cave resembles the female reproductive system, and the actual Birthing Cave mirrors a womb. For obvious reasons, this landmark on Mescal Mountain is called

"The Mother." This location not only represents physical births but spiritual rebirthing as well.

As our guide finished telling us about this site, I pulled up a map on my phone and dropped a pin. Later, I planned to explore the trail and learn how to reach this cave. My intuition urged me to visit this place before departing Sedona.

Our final stop was Airport Mesa. With easy access to the top of the mesa, the reward of impeccable views without much effort makes it a famous tourist destination. Airport Mesa is known for up-flow vortexes, which help you reach a higher level of consciousness and give you a higher perspective. Many will go to up-flow vortexes to meditate. On my prior visit to Sedona, I meditated at a specific vortex location at Airport Mesa, and when I opened my eyes, everything looked like snow on a TV screen. The gentleman guiding the meditation told me I was seeing the energy of everything around me. This was the first time I'd ever 'seen' energy, and it was an incredible experience.

As I stood on top of the mesa, the air was fresh, and the scent of rain lingered. I then thought about how this 3-hour experience related to life. I had experienced peace and solitude yet weathered the storm and witnessed a rainbow. In this short time, I experienced the metaphorical roller coaster of life. Remember that storms are an inevitable part of life, so look for the beauty and lessons within them, and don't forget to savor the rainbow afterward, the gift of the storm.

Our time had concluded as we headed down Airport Mesa and made our way back to our original meeting point, and we all departed our separate ways. My friend and I went to dinner and shared our individual experiences from the tour. We both agreed we felt connected to Mother Earth and Sedona's energy. We were eager for day two.

On the second day, waking up to rain meant we were forgoing outdoor activities, so we opted to go shopping and have an intuitive reading from a local spiritual advisor. These readings are valued for offering insights into one's future path. You can ask specific questions or openly receive what the reader intuitively shares.

After settling on our plan, I started searching for "best readers in Sedona," but stopped short. Over the years, I have developed a relationship with my spirit guides and spiritual team for advice and direction. While searching, they instructed me not to look for a specific person to see. Once I received this message, I informed my friend that we weren't meant to plan our day or schedule a reading with anyone in particular; instead, we should go with the flow. We would be guided to where and to whom to receive a reading from. She was fluid with this idea and agreed.

After a relaxing morning, we hopped into our car and headed into town. I requested guidance from my spirit guides to direct us to the place for our readings. As we approached Highway 89A, we entered a more populated area. During the drive, I spotted a crystal shop on the left and excitedly exclaimed while pointing, "Here it is! This is the place we're meant to stop!" My friend pulled in, parked the car, and we walked into the store.

A friendly woman welcomed us and inquired how she could assist. We both expressed interest in readings, and she provided a list of available readers. One of them approached us, and I felt an immediate connection. He was the reader my guides indicated for my session. He offered a "crystal casting" reading, a concept unfamiliar to me, but I was willing to try it. I requested a 30-minute session while my friend went to the shop next door.

He began by explaining the properties of each crystal he would use in the reading, along with the grid the crystals would be cast on. The grid is what we know as the Star of David; however, from a spiritual standpoint, it symbolizes how our inner and outer life merges, a template of the sky. (Think of a natal birth chart.) Each point and the space in between are related to specific areas of our life and how they are interconnected.

He then centered his energy, said a quick prayer, and cast the crystals on the board. Most of the Lemurian diamonds gathered in the center, which he said was unusual yet lovely. He began the reading by explaining where each crystal had fallen and its meaning to have landed within the certain area it did. One closest to the center suggested an acceleration of change, a sense of being reborn. "Was this why I felt so drawn to the Birthing Cave the day before, as it's a place of rebirth?" I thought. The next 6-8 months would be a time of reflection and making choices based on where I saw my life going. Then he went on to say if I was in a relationship, intimate and able to have children, be careful. This was a beautiful symbol of pregnancy. I smiled, laughed lightly, and said, "I just felt my abdomen jump when you said that!" I continued, "So if you want children, you're saying that's a good time?" "Yes," he said with a smile. "And if you don't want children, be very careful!" This message came through just three minutes into the reading. I found the timing of this message fascinating, considering my Husband and I had started discussing adding to our family just a few months prior since hearing a little girl's voice speak to me.

Although I had agreed to 30 minutes, the session lasted an hour. Little did the reader know the validation he gave me, or did he? Day two was another successful day in the books.

We woke up on day three with the sun shining and weather that seemed to give you a warm, comforting hug. It was the perfect day for another hike. Over coffee that morning, I told my friend I didn't need to make it an all-day adventure, but I wanted to hike Mescal Mountain and go to the Birthing Cave. She just wanted to spend the day outdoors again and didn't care which mountain we went to. We packed up and headed to where I dropped the pin location two days prior.

After arriving, we parked and located the trailhead. I snapped photos of the trail map of Mescal Mountain for reference during our hike. With no time constraints, we leisurely hiked around the mountain, captured pictures, and took breaks for water and snacks. While we rested to refuel, we heard music in the distance. Looking across the valley, we saw someone on a vortex site in Boynton Canyon playing a flute, surrounded by a small audience of hikers. We observed and listened from afar. Then, we each found a rock to sit on and meditated, letting the flute's melody drift over to us. When the flute music ended, we took it as a sign to continue our journey around the mountain, following the signs that guided us along the path.

Our Shamanic guide two days prior had mentioned the path to the Birthing Cave was off the regular trail and to look for a fence line. After hiking four miles, we still couldn't find any indication of the fence or "The Mother." I began to feel uneasy, worried that I had led us on a wild goose chase. After about another half mile, we discovered the ragged fence line just as he had described. We followed the narrow trail beside the fence, and, keeping our focus forward, we paused to look up. There was "The Mother."

At that moment, I told my friend it seemed like an appropriate time to be in silence. She agreed and hiked in silence alongside me.

While hiking, I felt compelled to reach out to the soul that had connected with me months earlier. I began an internal dialogue, engaging with her spirit telepathically and expressing my openness to her joining me on Earth, should she be ready. I also gently requested that she come when her dad would be home, as this had always been a significant concern for me. His travel schedule made me anxious about the possibility of him missing the birth if we were to have a child. As I continued our communication, I sensed her spirit drawing closer. With each step I took towards the womb at Mescal Mountain, it felt as if I was bringing her nearer to my womb.

In almost a hypnotic state, yet consciously aware of my decision, I looked up and noticed cutouts on the side of the cliff. I pointed to them and said, "Let's go over here." We deviated from the clear path to the womb and turned left to make our ascent to this secluded site.

We had to climb over a few boulders but made our way into one of the caves, which felt like it had summoned me. The ceiling of the cave was still charred from the fires that once burned to keep the Hopi women warm as they gave birth here. The energy of this cave was overwhelmingly magnetic, loving, and "motherly."

I sat in awe as I looked around the cave I was now nestled in. Chills covered my body. I gazed out into the horizon and wondered what it was like to hike to this site while pregnant, maybe even in labor, and to give birth here. "Such strong, brave, and incredible women." I thought to myself.

I then decided to record a quick video of my thoughts, while sitting in the cave. This trip reminded me several times that I had transformed into the grounded, peaceful person I had always aspired to be. I felt at that moment I had made it. I had officially stepped into the version of me I intended to become in this lifetime, and it felt so amazing. What a gift.

Once I recorded the quick video, I walked over to where my phone was placed and started to turn the camera off when I heard an overpowering message not to put it away but to record another video. I put my phone back down, hit record, sat back down on a rock in the cave that had become my chair, faced the camera, and began to speak. With tears cascading down my face, I looked at the camera and spoke directly to Aria. I told her I was ready, if she was ready to come here. I promised to keep her safe and to support her however she needed. I welcomed her into my womb.

Before putting my phone away, my friend took a picture of me creating a heart with my hands, holding my womb. I didn't know then how this raw and vulnerable moment recorded on September 14, 2022, would hold such a special place in my heart.

It was time to go home, back to reality. Once again, I had been sprinkled with Sedona's magic dust during this trip, but I had no idea of its magnitude at the time.

Three months later, it was the day of the winter solstice. After waking and having a few sips of my morning coffee, I looked at my husband and said, "I feel different." "What do you mean?" He asked. "I feel dizzy but not completely off kilt. It's hard to describe. I just feel different." With a puzzled look on his face, he tried to grasp my sense of feeling "different." I shifted the conversation, and we continued with our day.

Two days later, on December 23rd, our friends who had two young children and was expecting their third, were in town visiting family for Christmas, and chose to stay with us that night before returning home. While we stood in the kitchen chatting, I told her how I was feeling "different" and wasn't sure what to make of it. "Maybe since you're discussing starting a family, your body is getting ready for it." Her remark made sense to me as I recognized my body's intuition and the strength of the mind-body connection.

Her husband then walked over to interrupt our conversation gently. "After getting the work done on the car, we forgot to put the "baby kit" back in the trunk, leaving us with only two diapers." We looked at the time on the clock, and the grocery stores had already closed. "You don't have any diapers, do you?" She asked me. "Unfortunately not, but I have baby wipes I use for Lily after she plays in the grass. You're welcome to those." I responded with some resolution to their problem.

That night, when tucking into bed, I told my husband we should create a baby kit for our house consisting of diapers, wipes, pacifiers, and toys since most of our friends had children. He agreed. Before shutting off the lights to call it a day, I added a note to my "to-dos" to get the items when it was convenient.

The holiday season had come and gone. Now, in the new year, my husband received an invitation to a guys' dinner on January 9th. I suggested we carpool; I would drop him off before heading to dinner with a girlfriend.

On our way into the city for me to drop him off, there was an excessive amount of traffic. Every car, every light, every honk of a horn I heard seemed to aggravate me. This irritation then shed onto my husband, whom I told through my clenched jaw that if he did not stop telling me how to drive, I was going to reach over him, open the passenger door, and throw him out on the highway. "Gosh! That seems aggressive coming from you! Is everything okay?" he asked.

"I am fine. You are the issue right now. Stop telling me how to drive," I replied, still with my jaw clenched.

We reached the restaurant 15 minutes late, where the guys were already dining. I still needed to get to my girlfriend. On the way, the annoyance from every person and car increased my irritability. I was also extremely frustrated that I arrived at the restaurant I chose over 30 minutes late. As I sat down across from her, I sincerely apologized for my tardiness. She reassured me it was not a problem, mentioning she appreciated the extra time for herself.

After a fun evening catching up with friends separately, we drove home together. While I wasn't quite my usual calm self, I definitely felt more at ease than I had before our dinners.

Around 1 a.m., I was awakened from a deep sleep by the voice of my higher self saying, "Mel, stop drinking. You're pregnant." My eyes flew open, and chills coursed through me as I lay there in disbelief. "No way," I responded to my higher self. "We haven't been preventing it, but we certainly haven't been trying! I haven't kept track of anything!"

I eventually soothed my monkey mind by focusing on my breath and drifted back to sleep. The next morning, I woke up feeling confused but chose to keep this internal dialogue private, as I was still trying to make sense of it and had no evidence that what I heard was true.

Two nights later, during the wee hours of the night, my higher self woke me again and said, "You are pregnant. Take a test." I was stunned and thought, "What in the world? This is just crazy!" Unable to calm my racing thoughts, I lay there wide awake in confusion and shock. Eventually, I got up, grabbed my phone, and went to the guest room. I started researching pregnancy symptoms. Some matched what I had been experiencing, while others didn't. I opened my phone's calendar and counted backward to the night I suspected we might have conceived if what I heard was true. If it was accurate, my due date would be in September. "Great," I thought, "Right in the middle of a schedule that wouldn't be ideal for giving birth." I sighed.

After hours of researching pregnancy symptoms, I finally put my phone away. My exhaustion took over, and I fell back asleep.

The next day, I had a full day of Reiki sessions. When I called my husband late in the afternoon to tell him I was going by the grocery store, I asked what he would like me to make for dinner. One detail I did not mention to him was the pregnancy test I was going to buy. I wasn't trying to hide anything from him; I was in disbelief that what I was hearing was true and, honestly, I was feeling a little crazy. "How about a date night instead?" he asked. "That sounds like fun!" I replied. We discussed the details of where to go, and once I arrived home, I freshened up and out the door we went.

Once we arrived at our favorite restaurant, we watched a torrential thunderstorm as we sat outside on the covered patio. Moments later, we received alerts simultaneously on our phones about the tornado warning. Our poor dog, Lily, was home alone, so we each pulled up different weather apps on our phones to see how bad the conditions were. It was a little south of our home and closer to where we were having dinner, so we decided to keep an eye on the house and our dog through the cameras and call a neighbor if needed. If we left to go home, we would have to drive right through the storm, which we agreed would pose more of a threat than staying put.

We enjoyed the perfect date night filled with deep conversations, sharing personal highlights, and laughing at funny memories. After the rain had cleared, we drove home only to find our power was out. Once we arrived, my husband began setting up the generator until I said, "No! Let's light some candles, enjoy a nightcap, cuddle Lily on the couch, and stick to the theme of the evening. I'm really enjoying our conversations." He smiled, and we followed through with my idea.

The power came back on shortly after we settled in on the couch together. After finishing our nightcaps, we showered and drifted off to sleep. Around 2am my higher self came knocking away again, waking me up, but this time more forcefully than the past conversations. "Mel! Enough! No more drinking. You are pregnant! Get the test tomorrow. Stop waiting." I was literally being scolded. "Fine!" I said to myself angrily as I fell back to sleep.

The following morning, I handled some obligations before heading to the grocery store. I picked up items from my list and proceeded to the baby essentials aisle to start assembling the "baby kit" for our home. I grabbed a pack of wipes, diapers, and, finally, a pack of pregnancy tests. At the checkout, I placed my items on the conveyor belt and struck up a conversation with the friendly women there. The bagger asked, "How old is your little one?" In my head, I thought, "About eight weeks in my belly." Realizing my instinctive mental response, I gathered my thoughts, met the bagger's gaze, and said, "Oh! Those diapers and wipes aren't for us. We had friends visiting who needed some supplies, so we figured it'd be smart to have these essentials in case they needed them again. We don't have any children ourselves." She smiled, although a bit bewildered, at my lengthy explanation.

After paying for the groceries and swapping pleasantries, I pushed my cart through the automatic doors and as I was making my way to my car, I laughed out loud as I thought, "Ha! I would find out I am pregnant on Friday the 13th. How fitting!" As I continued to laugh at the potential situation, I loaded my car with the cart full of groceries and headed home.

I pulled into the garage, and my Husband came to greet me to help carry the groceries into the house. After bringing them all in, he returned to his office to continue what he was working on before I arrived. After putting away the groceries, I crept into our bathroom to finally take the pregnancy test. I followed the instructions, urinated on the stick, and set it on a tissue I had placed on the floor. I washed my hands and came back to look at the test. In that short amount of time, there was a clear-as-day positive sign on the test. My jaw dropped as the blood flushed to my face. I could not believe it. I just stood there staring at the test. My higher self was right.

After collecting myself, I realized I needed to tell my husband the exciting news. I was unprepared and always thought I would do something cute and memorable when it was time to share such monumental news like this. I quickly formulated a plan. I kept all the gift bags in my office closet, so I nonchalantly walked into my office and scrummaged through what I had. The only sufficient thing was a wine bottle gift bag. That would have to do. I walked back into our bathroom, wrapped the test in tissue, placed it in the bag, and added the decorative tissue paper.

It was finally time. I had intuitively known I was pregnant since December 21st, but I had been in denial. I picked up my phone, switched to video mode, and pressed record. With my phone held by my side and the "gift bag" in the other hand, I walked to my husband's office. He noticed me as I approached, looking up from his computer. Our eyes locked; I smiled and said, "I got something for you at the grocery store today." He seemed confused as I continued, "Take a look." "Why do you have your phone out?" he asked, reaching for the bag. "Just look!" I urged in a shaky voice, trying to hold back tears. We went back and forth, him asking why my phone was out, and I kept urging him to look in the bag. As he continued to delay looking into the bag that held the most exciting news we could ever imagine, I could no longer hold back my tears. Concerned, he stood up and continued to ask why I was crying as he tried to comfort me. "Is everything okay? What's wrong? Why are you crying? I'm not looking at anything until you tell me what's happening," he said, concerned. I couldn't stop the tears and kept asking him to look in the bag. "No. Not until you tell me what's going on!" he replied. "I think I'm pregnant!" I blurted out. "No! Really?" he said with enthusiasm in his voice.

The escapade of going back and forth about what was in the bag, why I was crying, me telling him I was pregnant, and him being excited but in disbelief seemed to last hours, but it was only minutes. Eventually, I pulled the test out of the bag and showed it to him. He looked at it and confirmed the test did, in fact, show a plus sign.

I called the doctor right away, as it was almost 5 pm on Friday, and told them I had a positive pregnancy test and needed to schedule an appointment. They just happened to have an opening on the upcoming Tuesday, the only day my husband was available that week to attend the appointment with me, and we took it. The timing was already working out in our favor.

After scheduling the doctor's appointment, we took photos of ourselves with the positive test. All night, we kept asking each other if 'this was really happening,' both with shock and excitement.

The next few days were restless, but Tuesday's long-awaited day had arrived. We entered the OBGYN's office and checked in, then were taken to the ultrasound room. The technician reviewed my file and looked at me with a perplexed expression. "Can you explain why you're here? I see you had an appointment next week regarding a cyst concern, but now you're here today because of a positive pregnancy test." She inquired. "Yes," I replied. "I scheduled that earlier appointment due to some pain on the right side of my ovary. In the past, I experienced painful ovarian cysts, and I felt that same familiar discomfort. Since we wanted to start trying to conceive, I thought it was best to get everything checked out, but now here we are with a positive test." I explained. "Got it," she responded. "That makes sense."

She provided an overview of the exam and left the room for me to change into the gown. A few minutes later, she returned and started the exam. "You know your body! You're right, there is a cyst on your right ovary since that's the one you ovulated from," she said. "Wow! That's so fascinating!" I replied.

My husband and I watched on the screen as she performed the exam. She measured my ovaries, and then there it was a little sac in my uterus indicating I was pregnant. She measured the sac and told me I measured at 6 weeks, not the 8 that I thought I was. If this was the case, when I knew I felt different but couldn't describe it, I was only two weeks pregnant.

After the exam, they scheduled another appointment for January 31st, a day before my departure to Sedona to host my first women's retreat. The wait of two additional weeks felt like an eternity.

On the night of the 18th, I woke up suddenly, thinking, "I feel different." I checked in with my body. Did this difference stem from the medical confirmation of my pregnancy? Was something wrong? I sensed a change, but I didn't need to panic. The reassurance my body provided that everything was okay helped me drift back to sleep.

The following day, I had a strong craving for pizza, so I opted for a cauliflower pizza and savored it while unwinding with some TV. My stomach was satisfied, and I felt completely at ease. Then, for a brief moment, I sensed what seemed like a heartbeat that wasn't my own. It lasted only a few seconds. Being highly attuned to energy, I often sensed things in clients before medical examinations confirmed my perceptions. I believed it was possible that, at that moment, I had felt my baby's heartbeat for the very first time.

That night, before going to bed, I enjoyed meditation and self-Reiki, my regular practice to help me relax at the end of the day. This time, I decided to play hertz frequency music for pregnancy in the background. During my self-Reiki session, I found myself connecting with the life growing in my womb. An overwhelming sense of masculine energy washed over me. "Oh my goodness, it's a boy!" I smiled, though confusion swept over me. Since I had heard Aria's voice back in July, I assumed I would have a girl and had been journaling to her. I started speaking to my baby, apologizing for mistakenly calling them a girl when they might be a boy. We still had months to wait for the bloodwork to confirm the sex. Regardless, I felt joy, and from that moment, I began our daily positive affirmations for the entire journey: "We are healthy. We are strong. We are vibrant."

CHAPTER 2

Why Reiki

Reiki is not only a healing modality I keep in my medicine cabinet to make boo-boos better; I've embodied it as a way of life. When I look back to my first introduction, the timing of my encounter with Reiki doesn't seem surprising. I didn't go looking for Reiki; Reiki found me. The Universe attracts what we need in divine timing, even when we aren't consciously seeking it.

When I was in my mid-twenties, I grew a keen interest in health and fitness. A few years earlier, I had experienced some unusual health issues for someone my age, like shingles and the sudden removal of my gallbladder without a clear diagnosis. This prompted me to embark on a journey to understand more about my body, and I was always fascinated by the mind's ability to communicate with the body.

My senior dogs, Roxie and Salem, needed extra care during this time, so I turned to chiropractic treatment to support them. I knew a fitness instructor from the gym who was also a veterinarian specializing in horses and dogs. I started taking my girls to her for chiropractic adjustments.

One afternoon, while she was adjusting my dogs, I noticed that she was wearing crystal bracelets on her wrist and complimented her on them. She then told me about a woman she had started seeing who did energy work. Unfamiliar with "energy work," I was intrigued, open-minded, and all ears.

As she continued to work on my dogs, she explained the details of her session to me. As I listened intently, it sounded like something I should try. I got the energy worker's contact information, reached out that afternoon, and scheduled an appointment about a week later.

When I arrived at her healing space, she greeted me with a smile, welcomed me in, and gestured for me to sit in a nearby chair. She then sat in her desk chair across from me and asked general questions about why I was there. I explained that my dog's chiropractor had shared her experiences with me, and I was fascinated by what she shared about her session, so I also wanted to try it.

After a few minutes of conversation, she briefly explained how she would conduct the session and what I might experience. She asked me to lie down on the massage table face up, fully clothed. During the session, there were times when she gently rested her hands in certain places, such as my shoulders, and other times when she hovered over my body. At moments, she would share information about what she felt or saw.

During the session, she placed her hands on the right side of my abdomen, on top of my liver. The heat from her hands slowly started to make me sweat, and that was when I began to cry uncontrollably. There was no conscious thought or memory to invoke the tears streaming down my face, and then, out of nowhere, I felt angry. As she continued to work on me, I felt the rumbles of anger stirring up even deeper, like the bubbling of hot lava rising in a volcano. I was drowning in the mucus from my nose and tears, while my body involuntarily quivered as I wept. Each tear shed felt connected to an event tucked away in a box, on a dark shelf in the back of a closet, called my subconscious mind.

I walked out of the session in an exhausted daze, my face red and swollen from crying. As I drove home in silence, I tried to sort through the events to help process what had just happened. I hadn't been aware of the emotions, especially anger, that I had been carrying all this time. I was still unsure what exactly I had been so angry about, but I felt a sense of relief.

I attended a few more sessions with her and eventually found The Nook in Davidson, NC, a community that hosted intuitive and mindfulness classes. It was also during this time that I began to meditate frequently to help manage my stress. From these intuitive classes and meditation practice, I cultivated a relationship with my Spirit Guides. In a meditation one night, I heard my Healer Guide say to me, "You can help heal your mom," and in my gut, I knew Reiki was the right direction.

Over the years, my mom struggled with leg pain and numbness that eventually affected her ability to walk. She was feeling defeated after undergoing numerous tests, MRIs, CT scans, spinal taps, and two invasive surgeries—one surgery involved replacing her C5 vertebra with a metal spacer and plate. Despite surgeries, medications, and physical therapy, she found no relief or signs of improvement.

The saying goes, "When the student is ready, the teacher appears." At the Nook, a Reiki Master with extensive training taught Reiki, sound baths, and other intuitive classes. I enrolled in her upcoming Reiki I and II training and became a Reiki Practitioner. Learning Reiki felt like a homecoming, as if I had been missing a part of myself without realizing it. It felt familiar, and every part of me remembered it. Right away, I began giving myself Reiki daily and continued to reap its benefits. I wanted the world to experience what I was, so six weeks after becoming certified, I opened my healing practice, SoulFull Co., and started seeing clients.

Within five months of seeing clients, I was already providing sessions for an average of 25 people per month. My Reiki business was experiencing remarkable growth, largely driven by enthusiastic word-of-mouth referrals. At this pivotal moment, I decided to elevate my practice and become a Reiki Master in February 2020, shortly before the global pandemic brought the world to a standstill.

During the challenging months when face-to-face meetings weren't possible, I offered distant Reiki sessions and organized complimentary online meditation sessions to help individuals cope with the mental strain caused by isolation and the overwhelming fear of uncertainty. As soon as I could resume in-person Reiki sessions, the demand was astonishing. The pandemic became a critical moment for many, prompting them to explore alternative methods to nurture their mental and emotional well-being. Reiki offered the comfort, assistance, and recovery they were seeking. I felt a deep sense of gratitude that they trusted me as the one to experience Reiki with.

During this period, I excitedly shared with my mom the amazing experiences I was having with Reiki and the positive effects my clients felt after just a few sessions. It was a special time for my mom as she was preparing for her wedding in October 2020. She was beginning to feel concerned that her physical limitations might overshadow her big day.

Now only in her mid-50s, she found it increasingly challenging to maintain her balance and mobility. Even walking was a struggle; she relied on a rollator for support. With her wedding approaching in just six weeks, she decided to explore Reiki feeling that she had exhausted all other options. In the lead-up to her big day, we scheduled regular Reiki sessions, aiming for at least once a week. Her aspirations were clear: she hoped to walk down the aisle, stand independently during the ceremony, and share a dance with her new, wonderful husband.

We followed through with her commitment to frequent Reiki. On the day of her wedding, I had the honor of walking my mother down the aisle without the assistance of a rollator. I proudly gave her away to her new husband and witnessed her standing confidently throughout the entire ceremony. As the evening unfolded, I watched her dance the night away in pure love and laughter. It was a testament to her unwavering determination and the profound impact of Reiki. Having personally witnessed the transformative power of Reiki in my mother's life, I gained a deeper understanding of its remarkable value. Despite years of discouragement and exhaustion from trying various methods, Reiki infused her with hope and delivered what seemed unattainable.

After witnessing the positive impact of Reiki on my mom's well-being and experiencing its intense effects in my own life, I felt inspired to pursue further knowledge and delve deeper into Reiki. A year after attaining the level of Reiki Master, I decided to enroll in a program to become a Certified Medical Reiki Master (CMRM) under the guidance of esteemed Raven Keyes. Renowned for pioneering the integration of Reiki into the operating room alongside top American surgeons such as Dr. Mehmet Oz and Dr. Sheldon Marc Feldman, Raven was at the forefront of introducing Reiki's holistic healing into mainstream medicine.

After obtaining my CMRM certification, I began working with a growing number of clients who were undergoing chemotherapy treatments, people who suffered from unexplainable conditions that hindered their quality of life, and women looking to conceive or who were expecting. This was when I began growing a greater understanding of how Reiki supported more than what was initially apparent.

Reiki had proven to me how trapped emotions affected my physical body, but witnessing my clients' revelations of gaining this understanding was sheer magic. Clients who had been plagued with unexplainable chronic ailments, such as migraines, gastrointestinal issues, and ongoing knee pain were experiencing relief for the first time since they could remember. Women who were told they would have trouble getting pregnant would then have a healthy, full-term pregnancy. Clients were sleeping better, performing better, and quickly noticing improved overall mood and outlook. The list of positive side effects Reiki was having on them was endless.

Once my husband and I decided to start a family of our own, I became even more thankful for the years of work I had done up to that point and the education I'd gained from hands-on experiences with clients. I had not only freed myself from the emotional baggage I had carried in my lifetime but also cleared the generational burdens that had been passed down to me. By doing this work, I provided a clean emotional canvas for my son. What a gift to him. This realization made me believe Reiki and the Universe were orchestrating a plan beyond my comprehension. I had followed this path with an open heart and mind, trusting in the guidance of forces greater than myself.

Not only has Reiki helped me heal from within by releasing stored emotions, but it's also provided a greater level of self-awareness, especially as a mother. Reiki has taught me to live in the present moment with a deep sense of grounding and empathy. It's helped me remain calm during inevitable stressful situations, especially when I was learning to navigate motherhood with my newborn son.

It allowed me to tune into what he needed and listen to what he communicated through his body language or cries.

It has enabled me to become a more compassionate and understanding person and a better wife and mother. The gift of Reiki is truly unparalleled, as it continues to grant its blessings endlessly. I've also found it is the perfect offering in moments of uncertainty, when words fail to convey our feelings, or when your physical presence is impossible, yet sympathy is needed; Reiki serves as the ultimate solace. I often remind my students that while they may occasionally overlook Reiki, it always remembers them. They can call on it whenever, wherever. During times of confusion or when support is essential, Reiki leads us back to our authentic selves, providing the comfort and guidance we seek.

Because of my experiences with Reiki I undoubtedly use it as a guiding force, but it also is a key presence in my home. Throughout my pregnancy, I turned to Reiki to cultivate a sense of calmness and assurance. As I channeled Reiki energy to my growing son within my womb, I experienced a deepening connection to the universal life force while fostering a powerful bond with him. While giving Reiki to him during my pregnancy, I noted every intuitive sensation and insight that came to me. It's remarkable how many of the things I wrote about his personality and my expectations for him have proven to be true so far. I also know Reiki was an essential component of me having a positive and healthy pregnancy and birthing experience.

Reiki was a wonderful way for me to strengthen my connection with my son while he was in the womb and has done the same for him now earthside. When I can tell he needs extra emotional support or a reset, Reiki is an additional menu item I turn to. It is also my go-to method when he's been sick or teething, particularly when he has had a fever. I'll give him Reiki before bedtime, and every single time, he wakes up the following day with the fever gone.

When I feel my cup getting empty, I pour myself some Reiki and all becomes well within my world again. It gets me out of my mind and back in my body, grounds me, and helps me realign and regroup when I need it, allowing me to show up better for myself and my family.

I've also developed the habit of giving myself Reik before bed. It's a way for me to unwind, let go of anything that may have caused me stress or anxiety during the day, and puts my body in a calm state for rest. I've noticed I sleep better, making me feel more vibrant the next day, especially during the early months of motherhood when I was running off of 3-4 hours of sleep a night.

Reiki has done wonders for me physically and emotionally, but it has also become a mindfulness practice. Every day, sometimes multiple times a day, I recite the Reiki precepts, also known as the Gokai, which are golden standards to live by. It says, "just for today, do not be angry, do not worry, be grateful, do your work/duties fully, be kind to others."

The Gokai is special to me because of the deep meaning behind the phrase "Just for today" in Japanese, which translates to "in this moment." This concept is a powerful reminder to pause, start over, and be present with everything I am and am not doing.

I've found that using these principles as a guide has helped me become kinder to myself, especially as I navigate through motherhood. Now, I take the time to observe my thoughts and actions and give myself grace, acknowledging that I'm only human and doing my best. Some days are tougher than others, and when I feel angry or defeated, I recite the Gokai to center myself.

As a mother, the weight of responsibility is immense. Concerns about your baby's feeding schedule, whether they have eaten enough, the anticipation of much-needed sleep, and the hope for their peaceful slumber infiltrate your thoughts. In these moments, I say the Gokai. This simple action serves as a mental reset, allowing me to release my worries, place my trust in the greater forces of the Universe, and make peace with the idea that whatever is meant to be will be.

In this book, I highlight the significance of gratitude, drawing from my own experiences of its beneficial effects. Gratitude serves as a powerful remedy for anger and worry, steering your thoughts in a more positive direction. There are countless reasons to be grateful. While facing postpartum depression and anxiety can be daunting, embracing gratitude might ease some of these struggles.

"Do your work/ duties fully" serves as a gentle reminder for self-compassion and grace when necessary. Various factors influence my daily performance, causing my "best" to fluctuate. By reciting the Gokai each day, I've become comfortable with this notion, understanding that I'm doing my best in each moment even when today's 'best' doesn't look like yesterday's best.'

"Be kind to others" should be the standard, yet it isn't always easy for everyone, especially when it comes to being kind to oneself. I believe kindness can manifest in many ways, like letting someone with fewer groceries go ahead in line or helping an elderly person cross the street. It also includes showing kindness to yourself in whatever way resonates with you. This is particularly important for those supporting new moms or expecting mothers, as they often struggle with self-identity due to hormonal changes, which can be quite challenging. Hence, extending kindness, along with patience, to them is crucial.

What I've shared only hints at Reiki's deep impact on my life yet highlights why I'm such a passionate advocate for everyone to learn it. Mother Teresa's quote, "I alone cannot change the world, but I can cast a stone across the water to create many ripples," embodies my feelings about teaching Reiki. It's my life's mission to spread this modality to anyone eager to learn, and empowering mothers through this knowledge generates a positive ripple effect, particularly benefiting their children.

Reiki and Children

Reiki provides numerous benefits to children, but it can also help them express to you what's going on in their bodies. I had just taught a long-term Reiki client Reiki I, and the following week, her six-year-old daughter had been complaining of stomach pain. She didn't have a fever, nor did she have vomiting or diarrhea, but after multiple days out of school, my student contacted me and asked for guidance. Being a newcomer to practicing Reiki, she asked the typical questions, "Am I doing it right?" and "How do I know it's working?" I confirmed that, in training, she connected with Reiki quickly and reassured her that she was doing everything 'right.' Although she was new to giving it, she had been receiving it from me for years. She was certainly no stranger to Reiki and its benefits.

During our conversation, she mentioned giving Reiki to her daughter before bedtime, which helped her sleep, though she continued to complain about stomach pain. I suggested that the next time she worked on her daughter, she should ask her to close her eyes and describe anything she saw. The following day, while treating her daughter again, my student followed this advice. Her daughter closed her eyes and said, "I see yellow." My student was taken back. Her daughter had no prior knowledge of Reiki, chakras, or the color associations, yet she immediately saw yellow, the color linked to the Solar Plexus — precisely where her stomach pain was localized.

After further discussions and evaluations with her six-year-old, my student realized her daughter's anxiety had significantly increased, causing the stomach pain. By incorporating more Reiki and discussing her daughter's emotional state, her stomach pain improved. My student aimed to learn Reiki I to benefit herself and her family, and she accomplished just that. Years later, she continues to practice Reiki on herself and her family regularly. Reiki not only empowered this mother to get to the root cause of her daughter's discomfort, but it helped her child sleep.

Everyone can appreciate a good night's rest, and a long-time client and friend was eager to learn Reiki specifically to cater to her children. Given my experience of working with children, I concentrated on teaching her how to implement a more unconventional approach to giving her child a treatment. Reiki can be given to a child while they're coloring, eating, cuddling, or watching TV. The day after completing my weekend Reiki training and becoming a Certified Reiki Practitioner, this mama wasted no time applying Reiki with her son.

The following evening, as her three-year-old sat down for dinner, she decided to perform a Reiki session to help him relax. Her husband observed with curiosity and inquired about her actions. "I'm hoping to help him sleep better tonight," she confided quietly. Their son had only experienced uninterrupted sleep once for six hours, at 20 months old. Sleep had been a persistent challenge in their household, with their son waking up as many as four times a night and requiring either her or her husband to soothe him back to sleep.

Surprisingly, that night, their son drifted off within 20 minutes, a process that typically took over an hour, often causing her husband to fall asleep during it. With fingers crossed, they retired for the night.

On the first night, their son woke up only once, and he quickly fell back asleep. His first night went so well she decided to give her son Reiki again before bedtime the next night. Once more, he fell asleep swiftly, but this time, he slept through the entire night. For the first time since his birth, he enjoyed a solid 10 hours of sleep, allowing them to get a complete night's rest as well. Sleep is precious; any parent who has faced sleep deprivation will resonate with this experience.

Reiki is not only beneficial for younger children, but I have also discovered it to be very effective for pre-teens and teenagers. Today's younger generation appears to be more empathic and intuitive, requiring supportive and conscious parents. (More on this later in the book.) Although it is a gift to have more sensitive children coming into the world, without a solid understanding of their feelings, children can become overwhelmed by mixed emotions, often unaware of the reasons behind them. When these emotions linger, they can cause significant distress in their developing bodies, manifesting as unexplainable physical symptoms and increased anxiety.

Sue had been urgently looking for help for her two daughters. One day, she searched for 'Energy Medicine' and found my website. While she was somewhat familiar with Reiki, she didn't know many details. She shared my website with her seventeen-year-old daughter, Emily, who is very intuitive. Emily felt I gave her 'good vibes' rather than 'witchy' ones and decided to try a session with me.

Sue contacted me to set up her appointment. When she and Emily arrived, Sue was in tears. Her voice trembled as she spoke, tears softly streaming down her face. She explained how they had taken Emily to the doctor repeatedly, only to have her symptoms dismissed as hormonal. Although medication was prescribed, it had been ineffective. Emily was completely drained, suffering from intense anxiety, depression, headaches, and insomnia. Sue's motherly intuition told her something was 'off,' and she needed to explore other options for Emily.

In our session, I asked Emily targeted questions based on my observations of her energy body. It became clear that this young woman was highly empathic, so I explained what that entailed. I suspected that her symptoms stemmed from absorbing others' energy; her emotional reservoir was full and overflowing, making it difficult for her to distinguish her feelings from those around her. I provided her with 'energy homework' and guided her on how to start nurturing herself energetically. After our session, Emily appeared a bit lighter, had a glimmer in her eye, and even smiled at me. I was confident we were heading in the right direction.

She agreed to see me every other week in the beginning and enjoyed our sessions so much that she encouraged her younger sister, Sophie, who was fourteen, to begin seeing me as well. Sophie was also suffering from low energy, had low self-esteem, and was experiencing frequent panic attacks.

Over several months of consistent Reiki sessions, Emily and Sophie experienced remarkable transformations. They appeared to radiate a newfound lightness and calmness, exuding a sense of confidence that was previously absent. Emily gained a profound awareness of the impact of others' energies on her well-being, prompting her to reevaluate her social circle and prioritize safeguarding and purifying her own energy. Witnessing the profound changes in her daughter's behavior and health, Sue decided to pursue all three levels of Reiki training with me, becoming a Reiki Master herself. Sue implemented a regular Reiki routine for herself, embarking on a journey of releasing generational imprints, leading to a transformative shift in her perspective on life and a deepening of her bond with her daughters.

Emily felt an abundance of energy, prompting her to pursue an early graduate plan, which she successfully completed. Her confidence led her to enroll in an out-of-state college. Now thriving in college, she enjoys a wonderful circle of friends and has even adopted a dog. Meanwhile, in her senior year of high school, Sophie is excelling academically, maintaining good health, and beaming with vitality.

I had the pleasure of working with Emily and Sophie for almost a year until I went on maternity leave. Both of these remarkable young ladies have drastically changed since our initial session. Sue also shares her eternal gratitude for Reiki's positive and lasting effects on her daughters and herself. I am thankful Reiki brought us together, and I enjoy receiving updates every so often on how everyone is doing.

Being a mother often requires resourcefulness. While one might not choose to learn Reiki seeking external support reveals so much. When a child has a family member, especially a parent, battling an illness like cancer, the impact is devastating. I've observed children completely withdraw when a loved one faces such challenges, as they often find it hard to process their emotions. They worry that their parent or loved one may not be around as long as they hoped, and this harsh reality can be overwhelming to handle without outside assistance.

Nicole's sister, a close friend and client, prompted her to experience Reiki. In November 2021, Nicole visited me for her first Reiki session. Diagnosed with terminal stage four metastatic triple-negative breast cancer, she was willing to explore any options to ease her anxiety before chemotherapy and help manage her pain. Her daughters, Faith, sixteen, and Hope, eleven, were also experiencing significant anxiety due to their mother's diagnosis and the limited time doctors had predicted for her survival.

In Nicole's initial session, we talked about the significant role mindset and energy would have in her breast cancer journey. After a few Reiki sessions and implementing the techniques I shared, she noticed a shift in her perspective, experiencing an inner peace she hadn't felt since her diagnosis. This acknowledgment helped her realize how her energy influenced her daughters. Eager for them to find the same relief she had, Nicole encouraged her daughters to explore Reiki, too.

Each month, Reiki evolved into a family tradition. They all became hooked on the positive feelings it brought, even amidst Nicole's frequent hospital visits. Their anxiety subsided as they spent more time connecting with nature and journaling, which helped them process their emotions rather than suppress them and lash out. Nicole began to realize how the emotional scars from her lifetime had manifested physically, and as a protective mother, she wanted her daughters to avoid the same experiences. They all dedicated themselves to more energy self-care practices, and the best outcome was the strengthened bond they developed through doing it together.

I physically got to hug Nicole for the last time in January 2023. She gave the best hugs. Even though I won't have the opportunity to hug her again, her light and spirit will forever hug my heart. Nicole outlived her doctor's expectations by over a year. Before she transitioned in March 2023, she expressed her deep belief that Reiki and the power of prayer extended her time on this earth. That extra time with her family was truly invaluable.

I continued to work with Faith and Hope to support them through grieving the loss of their mother. Although Reiki wouldn't magically erase their pain, it aided them in processing their emotions, providing a degree of peace during this profoundly devastating time. I know their mama is proud of them for their strength and determination to continue to heal and still watches over them.

Reiki is a gift available to everyone and has become a staple in my household, just as it has for many others. I'm thankful to have been led to this modality, which helped me release stored emotions that had affected me physically, granted my mother the opportunity to shine on her wedding day, and transformed the lives of many Reiki clients and their children. But how does Reiki really work?

CHAPTER 3

Reiki and the Physical Body

In 1869, Russian chemist Dimitri Mendeleev began developing the periodic table. As he arranged chemical elements by their atomic mass, he left open spaces for additional elements that he believed would eventually be discovered, and he was right. Over time, more elements were revealed, completing the periodic table. Our exploration of Reiki and its history, along with the data gathered from scientific studies now being performed, will continue to disclose more information and fill in the blanks, just like the periodic table.

With Reiki continuing to grow in popularity, I look forward to it becoming the first course of action versus the last resort. This non-invasive, holistic modality is now offered as an integrative therapy method to complement traditional medicine. In my practice, Reiki has helped clients overcome infertility and has supported expectant mothers along with many children. Research indicates that Reiki is effective in reducing pain and alleviating stress and anxiety, making it a wonderful practice to embrace, particularly during times when you're looking to conceive and during pregnancy, birth, and motherhood.

Those unfamiliar with Reiki may feel apprehensive to try it because they don't understand it. To those new to Reiki, I often describe it as acupuncture without needles. Reiki addresses your entire body's chi (energy), which balances the energy that sustains all living beings. (We will explore this further in the next chapter on the energy body.) By balancing your chi, Reiki restores your energy to homeostasis, the equilibrium necessary for proper body functioning. The autonomic nervous system (ANS) is comprised of the sympathetic nervous system (fight or flight) and the parasympathetic nervous system (rest and digest). In homeostasis, our parasympathetic nervous system is driving the bus. Therefore, you are experiencing Reiki's balancing act. When the body is balanced, dis-ease cannot exist within you.

Picture yourself cruising down the highway in your car and noticing it pulling to the left. You take a moment to assess the situation, concluding that your car is likely out of alignment. As a result, you proactively schedule an appointment with the local mechanic. After a thorough assessment, the mechanic confirms that your car is indeed out of alignment and follows the necessary procedures to realign your car, ensuring that it drives smoothly and as intended. After the work is completed, you hop back in and head home, as it drives like new again. On the contrary, if you had continued to drive it while out of alignment, you would cause damage to the car, much like pushing your body while out of energetic alignment, causing varying degrees of damage to yourself.

Imagine if we took the time to care for our bodies as diligently as we do our cars. Consider Reiki as the skilled mechanic for your body, ensuring that every part is firing on all cylinders, allowing everything to function at its best. The overall goal is to keep our vessel in alignment at all times.

We've all heard the expression, "An apple a day keeps the doctor away," but I believe that "Daily Reiki keeps the doctor away." No matter how healthy we may be, we constantly expose our bodies to toxins from the air we breathe, the food we consume, and the products we apply to our skin. Additionally, negative thoughts and intense emotions such as anger and worry contribute to the accumulation of toxins in the body.

Imagine panning for gold as you sift the pan back and forth. The sediments gently fall through the fine grates, leaving behind the treasured gold. Similarly, think of Reiki as the action of sifting the pan back and forth, oscillating your cells rapidly, helping to sift away energetic and emotional debris and toxins. This then enters your blood, urine, lymphatic system, and gastric juices, ultimately being detoxified and eliminated by the appropriate organs.

By consistently nurturing your body and eliminating these toxins, you remove the barriers that disrupt the flow of energy, ultimately restoring energetic alignment. This allows your body to achieve homeostasis, the state of optimal health, including sexual and reproductive health.

In my work with clients facing infertility, I found various factors hindering their aspirations. Frequently, the stress of trying to conceive would burden their energy, compounded by fears that they might never achieve their goal. Sometimes, we would identify anxieties about the uncertainties of motherhood, and in certain instances, we would uncover unprocessed emotional scars from their past. A few I recall were feeling neglected as a child, sexual abuse, anger from various situations, and not feeling worthy.

When a woman doesn't conceive right away, many jump to the conclusion they will need IVF. Although, I'm grateful this is a viable option for many wanting to conceive who are having difficulties. If you find yourself in this position, I encourage you to explore your energy and emotional body; more information will be shared on these topics in the upcoming chapters. Once my clients and I identified their roadblocks, Reiki supported clients in moving past them, bringing their dreams of becoming mothers as their reality. I believe it can do the same for you.

Not only does Reiki support women looking to conceive from an emotional and energetic perspective, but it also works with the fundamental system in your body called the endocrine system. The main constituents of the endocrine system include the ovaries, pituitary gland, thyroid, and adrenal glands. The endocrine system is directly linked to multiple facets of your reproductive system, so utilizing Reiki can keep the energy flowing through these areas for optimal sexual reproduction and function.

Reiki works collectively with your ovaries and thyroid when you want to conceive. If your hormone levels are low, your fertility rate is impaired because your hormones interfere with the release of an egg from your ovary. This is why incorporating Reiki in your daily routine is vital when you're ready and attempting to conceive. An example of an emotion or mindset that can affect your thyroid is, "You never get to do what you want or feel you need to do and are always putting others before your own needs." In the chapter 'The Butterfly Effect, ' I will share more about the importance of self-nurturing before conception.

The endocrine system is also involved in growth, and the thyroid produces a hormone that helps your child's brain development. Reiki grants you the opportunity to optimize your child's energy flow in utero to support their healthy development and once they are outside the womb. This allows you to be an integral part of your child reaching milestones within your womb and beyond.

The pituitary gland is another essential part of the endocrine system during pregnancy. This tiny gland at the brain's base produces a hormone called prolactin. During pregnancy, this hormone signals to your body to have breast tissue grow and begin milk production for breastfeeding. These inner workings are excellent in helping you provide for your baby once they are born. Yes, your body needs an elevated prolactin level to support the new life you welcomed. However, if you are aware of having a thyroid imbalance already, this can also increase your prolactin level. If levels reach too high, this wreaks havoc on your emotional system, contributing to those unwanted and upsetting mood swings.

Also in the endocrine system are your adrenal glands, which are two triangular glands, one on each kidney. These small but powerful glands produce steroid hormones called cortisol and adrenaline. They are responsible for your blood pressure, immune system, and stress response. Keeping your stress moderate throughout your journey of trying to conceive and during pregnancy is necessary. Not only does your baby feel your stress while in utero, but you also want to keep your immune system strong and keep a healthy blood pressure rate to support you and your baby. Excessive cortisol can also hinder your labor progress. Reiki during labor can be highly beneficial, as it activates the parasympathetic nervous system, soothing pain and helping your body relax. This allows you to welcome your bundle of joy into the world with calmness and confidence.

As for the 4th trimester, keeping up with a regular Reiki practice is just as important as when you were trying to conceive or while pregnant, if not more. It will aid in your recovery, help you with pain management, and assist you in sleeping when you do have the opportunity to. When giving birth, your body undergoes the most significant swing in hormones. Although becoming a mother is a delight, adjusting to the changes of motherhood can be tiring, and there's no need to add more to your plate because of unnecessary imbalances.

Reiki not only supports you throughout your journey of motherhood and beyond, but it also aids your child during illness. As a mother, you aim to nurture and support your child for a quick recovery once they become sick. The most powerful medicine for a mother is Reiki, infused with a healing intention.

When my son was only eight weeks old, we received confirmation he had contracted RSV. Luckily, our pediatrician assured us his lungs were clear, and his oxygen levels were good, but they provided additional information on what to watch for and the signs we would need to take him to the emergency room.

Along with giving him saline drops and sucking out his nose with the Nozebot, sitting with him in the shower to help him breathe became a priority. Before we would get in together, I would put a few drops of eucalyptus oil on the floor, turn the shower knob up to the hottest setting and let the steam build before we'd enter.

While holding him skin-to-skin in my arms, I took some deep breaths, inhaling the lightly scented steam and exhaling as I felt our bodies relaxing together. Regulating my nervous system regulated his. I began talking to him and asking him to mirror my breaths as if he fully understood my healing intention, which I believe he did. I noticed him taking soothing breaths just as I was. Knowing his love for music and me singing to him, I made up a playful song and began to sing it in a rhythmic tune of Where is Thumbkin. "All this sickness, all this sickness, is not welcome; is not welcome. It's time for you to leave now; it's time for you to leave now. Wash away. Wash away." As

I sang, I held him with one arm and used my other hand to hold the washcloth and gently squeeze water over him, visualizing the water washing the RSV away.

After a bit of playtime singing, I took some more deep breaths, grounded myself, and called in my Guides and Angels, along with my son's, and said the Gokai to ignite the power of Reiki. As I held him in my arms and gave him Reiki, I talked to his body aloud, kindly asking it to release what was no longer serving him for his highest and best and asked it to leave. I then visualized and told my son to visualize a bright white light coming in through the crown chakra, penetrating every cell of his body, rejuvenating it, and invoking healing. I continued using the washcloth to squeeze water over his shoulders and body as I set the intention of the water rinsing everything down the drain. As I envisioned the healing white light and Reiki restoring the cells of his body, I said again aloud, "We are rinsing away all the sickness and watching it go down the drain. You are healthy, you are strong, you are vibrant."

I was unexpectedly surprised when he had a bowel movement at that moment and appreciated being in the shower. I laughed heartily as I expressed gratitude to Reiki, our Guides, and Angels for the healing that occurred. After cleaning us both up and putting a fresh diaper on him, I joined him in bed for more skin-to-skin contact. Just two days later, he had made significant progress, and by the fifth day, he had returned to his usual self.

Skin-to-skin care, also referred to as "Kangaroo care," is always wonderful as it produces oxytocin for you and your baby. Not only does it deepen your bond, but it can help your baby feel better, too. It stabilizes their heartbeat and breathing, regulates their temperature, and helps them feel safe, which can reduce their crying. If your child becomes sick and you're still breastfeeding, you can feed them more often as your breast milk contains antibodies, stem cells, white blood cells, and protective enzymes that help fight infection and speed up their recovery.

Even though my son was only eight weeks old, I felt including him in the process was important. I believe babies understand much more than we give them credit for. Especially if your child is old enough to participate in their healing, teach them early how to connect and communicate with their body. Make it playful as you instill this tool to teach them to invest in their health and themselves. Your child will inevitably get sick, especially in the first year, as their immune system builds, so incorporating Reiki is an excellent way to help your child feel better faster. Of course, I always recommend you be under the advisement of your pediatrician so they can have you keep an eye on what to look for in case symptoms escalate and your child needs medical attention.

How Reiki Works

Reiki has an incredible impact on your and your child's overall health and the function of your sexual health, but how does Reiki work?

Reiki is the Universal Life Force Energy that is accessible to everyone. This energy originates from a 'Source,' which may represent God, the Universe, or your higher self—whatever resonates with you. What sets a Reiki practitioner apart from those who provide alternative hand-healing methods is their receipt of an attunement from a Reiki Master. This attunement is a sacred process that means "activating the soul," making it possible to channel Reiki energy. It opens the Hara Line in the individual, linking to your strongest, vital energy center in the body known as the Tanden, which is situated two fingers below the navel.

The attunement process varies for each individual, just as becoming attuned to different levels of Reiki does. Some may feel warmth, while others might sense coolness or chills. Students have reported sensations of tingling in their bellies, where the Tanden is located. Emotional releases are also a common experience. One student shared that they were overcome by an overwhelming wave of love from God, a sensation they had never experienced before. Others might feel dizzy or light-headed as they process the surge of energy flowing through them. While it's not frequent, a few students have undergone a detox phase after their attunement, as their bodies adjusted to the elevated energy vibration, expelling what was no longer beneficial to them. However, like my experiences after attunements, most students immediately experience positive benefits from their attunement, including increased energy, better sleep, mental clarity, and healing of physical ailments.

After receiving the attunement, you can tap into this Universal Life Force energy anytime. When invoked, Reiki flows from your crown chakra to your hands, allowing you to share it with yourself, others, plants, animals, food, or anything in need of it. I ensure my students recognize that while giving Reiki, they are simply facilitators, serving as vessels for the energy to flow through. In my teachings, I liken Reiki to other skills: the more you practice and engage with it, the more at ease you'll feel when working with it.

How does receiving Reiki feel?

Before starting a Reiki session with a new client, I always take the time to explain the process. Each practitioner brings their own style to their sessions, so I make sure to outline what they can expect from mine. I let clients know that I work intuitively and ask if they would like me to share any messages I receive from my Guides, Angels, and their own Guides during the session. Every client has responded positively, and being able to share these personal insights has enriched my sessions. By using my intuition and flowing with where the energy in their body takes me, I can uncover hidden aspects within a client, helping them connect the dots to experiences stored in their bodies. This synergy of Reiki and traditional therapy is something I deeply appreciate, as it often leads clients to those "ah-ha" moments that enable progress with their therapists and future therapy sessions. I've also tapped into emotions deeply buried within a client's body. These emotions disrupt their energy flow, resulting in physical ailments and even diseases. We will explore this topic further in the next chapter.

When I guide clients through their first Reiki session, I explain that there's no right or wrong way to experience it. Each individual is unique, which means their session will also be one-of-a-kind, just like all sessions after that. Some clients see shapes, colors, or even vivid images. Others may feel sensations like pins and needles in specific areas of their bodies, while some have grumbling stomachs as energy flows through them. Emotional blockages may lead to an emotional release of pent-up feelings. I've had clients experience a sudden surge of energy jolting through them, and some instinctively want to shake out an arm or leg, signaling that stagnant energy needs to be released. A session's most common side effect is deep relaxation, as many fall asleep. Although it's highly rare, if a client doesn't have any of the experiences above, I validate they are still receiving the healing effects of Reiki. Each client who didn't 'feel or see' anything during their session reported they finally got a restful night's sleep, reassuring them that 'something' occurred.

Some practitioners opt for silence during sessions to enhance relaxation; however, I allow my clients to choose. If they prefer to zone out, I support that. Yet, I notice that first-time Reiki clients often have questions, and I urge them to ask. This approach tends to help clients relax further, enabling them to connect better with their bodies instead of staying in their heads. Talking throughout the session does not hinder the flow of Reiki going through me to them.

As you've learned in these two chapters on Reiki, it is an empowering tool to combat imbalances, allowing you to show up as the best version of yourself physically, emotionally, mentally, and spiritually. As a mother, I can attest to how time can be limited, and it has become ingrained in women that we must sacrifice ourselves to help others, especially our families. Mama, this couldn't be further from the truth, so start honoring yourself with little nuggets of Reiki as a small self-care routine; it will do wonders for you, I promise. You cannot pour from an empty cup. Trust me, I tried, and it doesn't work.

When instituting Reiki as a regular practice, you lead by example for your family, especially your child, as they are watching how you care for yourself and will follow in your footsteps. Your energy and how you show up affects them. Let's explore this further in the next chapter.

CHAPTER 4

Your Energy Body

Energy is the unspoken language of existence and is contagious. This chapter will break down multiple layers of this concept so you can innovatively understand your energy body. Take your awareness past your physical body senses, which you have come to define as your reality, and bring forth the consciousness that you are so much more than what meets the eye. You will now begin to tune into the frequencies within and around you and know they exist even though you may not physically see them.

Quantum physics, the fundamental study of matter and energy, has taught us everything is energy and carries its own vibration. Your physical body is comprised of tiny particles called atoms, which are broken down into subatomic particles: neutrons, protons, and electrons. Found in the center of each atom, the nucleus consists of neutrons, which do not carry a charge, and protons, which give a positive charge. The particles orbiting around the nucleus are called electrons. Each electron discharges its own negative charge of electricity. The variations in charge cause interactions among atoms resulting in an electromagnetic force. These atoms that create your makeup are vortices of energy that are spinning and vibrating, each one emitting its unique frequency. Not only are these atoms radiating energy, but they absorb energy as well.

Physicists have proven how two people or objects on the other side of the world, or the Universe, can have an energetic connection and impact each other. This is called "Quantum Entanglement". The Noble Prize for Physics was awarded to physicists for their research showing that particles, which are light years apart, still influence each other. If these particles can affect each other on opposite sides of the world and even light years away, it seems only logical to believe that energy close by would have the same impact.

Understand that vibrating atoms make up your physical body generating your unique frequency, the resulting energy flows through centers in your body called chakras. Chakra is the Sanskrit word meaning "wheel, vortex, or disk." Along with these atoms, you have "wheel" energy centers that are also vortices of energy spinning clockwise and counterclockwise. These energy centers reside in a line along the spine, radiate your energy frequency outward, and receive and store information coming inward. For this book, we will focus on the seven main chakras: The Root, Sacral, Solar Plexus, Heart, Throat, Third Eye, and Crown.

The Chakras

Physiologically, you cannot separate the mind from the body; it is intrinsically connected, and scientific studies have now shown how emotions affect the physical body. Because of this, an imprint of every important or emotionally significant event you have experienced is recorded in your chakras. Think of your charka system as an energetic blueprint, and every emotion you feel correlates to at least one, if not multiple, chakras. Along with your mind and emotions creating energetic blueprints in your energy centers, the energy around you affects your chakra system. When you take in the energy from those you encounter, you take in the emotion attached to it.

A "Healthy" chakra rotates in a clockwise direction, radiating your vibrational energy outward. Simultaneously, each chakra is spinning counterclockwise, absorbing everything around you. Due to the counterclockwise movement of the chakras, these wheels draw external elements into your chakras, allowing these outside influences to become a part of you.

If you've ever had a session with an energy worker, they may have used the terms "sluggish, blocked, or closed" to describe a chakra's energy. Think of sitting in traffic on the highway. You're far from being able to drive the posted speed limit, but you're slowly moving to your destination. This is how I view sluggish energy; it's still moving, just not at the speed it should be. The flow of energy depends on the amount of energetic congestion in the area.

What makes a "healthy" chakra "unhealthy" and become imbalanced, wreaking havoc on the energy body and, in turn, creating dis-ease in the physical body? Many circumstances can play a part in shifting the health of these energy centers, making them sluggish. Let me explain in more detail by sharing information about each chakra, its functionality, and examples of how conditions and outside influences can change your chakra blueprint.

Your Root Chakra is located at the base of your spine, your perineum. The emotions often associated with this chakra are feeling connected to the earth, survival, and safety and security.

Trauma is one of the most dominant factors I encounter in my practice, leading to an imbalance in the root chakra. Trauma encompasses anything that results in mental, emotional, or physical distress. Such disruption hinders this energy center because the experience upsets your sense of safety.

Moving forward, you'll notice that I've removed the term "trauma" from this book. To me, the term carries a negative association that keeps me anchored to the past, leaving me in a victimhood mindset. I aim to align with the energetic state I desire, so I refer to this concept as "emotional imprint." You acknowledge that these events occurred, yet they do not define you. The phrase "emotional imprint" conveys your awareness of your feelings attached to what you've faced but emphasizes that these emotions do not shape your identity.

Whether fully recognized or not, everyone has experienced some type of emotional imprint. No one's imprint is inferior to another's, and everyone handles, responds, and processes it in their own way. I have also learned that each person's stress level varies, affecting how they process their imprints. Some can only handle a saucer-sized amount of stress, others a plate, and some a platter-sized amount. Those who can handle a platter-sized amount of stress may unintentionally discount the stress or emotional imprint of someone who can manage the saucer-sized amount. For both individuals, the size of the situation feels the same. The magnitude of an incident is relevant to how that person perceives their stress weight limit. It is all applicable to that person.

Emotional imprints affect more than just the Root Chakra. I've encountered emotional imprints affecting the energy centers from the Root to the Throat. The emotional imprints stored in chakras create lower vibrations, making the once-healthy wheel sluggish because it is not a positive vibrational match.

When emotional imprints are not processed or released, imbalances remain in the body. From what I have encountered in my practice, unprocessed imprints can have an impact on your ability to conceive and to regulate your emotions during and after pregnancy. I tell clients, especially those looking to conceive, to get familiar with their energy body as it carries a lot of power in their overall well-being.

The Sacral Chakra is located at the first lumbar, to the top of the pelvic bone, and up to the naval. For women, this chakra is important as it houses the womb. This energy center is related to relationships, emotions, mental confidence, intimacy, passion for life, and creativity.

Unprocessed emotional imprints can greatly influence the sacral chakra. Depending on the imprint, you may struggle to share and feel secure enough to be intimate, both emotionally and physically. In my practice, I have noticed that this struggle may lead to challenges and delays in conception. Another common factor I have observed in clients that causes physical imbalances is the use of artificial substances, like birth control, to manage hormones. While I don't dismiss the use of birth control, it's essential to recognize that your body is designed to operate fully with all functions active. If you're facing hormonal disruptions or irregularities in your menstrual cycle, remember that your body is trying to communicate with you for a reason. Consider these questions to help identify the energetic root of imbalances: Is there challenging energy from a past imprint that needs processing and healing? Do I feel comfortable expressing my sexual desires? Am I in a relationship that is physically, emotionally, or mentally abusive or controlling, whether with a family member or partner? If you answer yes to any of these, I urge you to seek the necessary help and support.

The Solar Plexus Chakra is located between your navel and rib cage. This energy center is fundamental to your identity, serving as the center of raw emotions, self-esteem, and intuition. We've all heard the phrase "listen to your gut"? That's exactly why.

Since the Solar Plexus houses many of your organs for survival, including the liver, gallbladder, spleen, stomach, pancreas, diaphragm, and kidneys, unprocessed emotional imprints can become stuck here since this is the center of your raw emotions. Heavy hitters such as anger, resentment, fear, guilt, and unworthiness will trap in this chakra and cause many imbalances within the body. The two primary emotions I see in my practice that can make it difficult to conceive or create a more challenging pregnancy are anger and fear.

I've assisted clients in processing their feelings through Reiki, particularly anger toward someone who has left an emotional and challenging mark on their life. It is crucial, both emotionally and energetically, to work through these feelings by choosing a healing modality, whether it be Reiki or another form of therapy. I've observed that anger frequently surfaces in women facing challenges with conception. I can deeply empathize with the heartache and disappointment that accompany such struggles. From an energetic perspective, it's vital to recognize that this anger can create significant blocks in this energy center.

Fear is a genuine emotion for many, particularly when facing motherhood. Questions like, "What if I can't conceive?" "Will I be a good parent?" and "What if complications arise during my pregnancy?" can provoke anxiety. Additionally, after your baby arrives, fears and worries often persist. The fear of the unknown can burden your energy significantly. I will discuss fear further when we address mindset later.

The Heart Chakra is located at the center of the chest. It guides us in surrendering to the divine, practicing forgiveness, and processing our emotions related to our inner experiences. Attempting to control outcomes, especially during conception, pregnancy, and birth, can disrupt the balance of the Heart Chakra. By trusting that a higher power is guiding you, whether that's the Universe, Source, God, or your Higher Self, you can calm the energy around and within you throughout this journey. Tools will be given in this book to help you attain this inner peace and contentment.

If you have unresolved emotional imprints, this energy center may be impacted. It can lead to feelings of distrust towards others, preventing your heart from being open to receiving love. These imprints can also influence your capacity to forgive. I encourage clients to understand that forgiveness is not for the other person but for themselves. Ultimately, forgiveness enables you to move forward personally, which brings more harmony to your energetic well-being.

The Throat Chakra serves as a vital energy hub associated with all aspects of life. It embodies truth, communication, harmony with others, and self-expression. An emotional imprint may influence this energy center, especially if you experienced difficulty voicing your feelings about the event.

The most common cause I see for someone experiencing an imbalance in the Throat Chakra is that they don't speak up for themselves; however, this may be due to another imbalance in a different chakra. For example, if someone has felt unsafe for most of their life, they may not speak up and advocate for themselves due to the fear of what may happen afterward. This example affects three chakras: not feeling safe, the Root; fear of repercussions from speaking up, the Solar Plexus; and not using their voice, the Throat.

Negative or toxic thoughts and words can disrupt your chakra system. Each thought or word generates an electric current, and if that current stems from negativity, it adversely impacts your energy centers. Conversely, positive thoughts and words can enhance your energy centers. This influence is particularly significant during conception, pregnancy, and postpartum. I'll elaborate more on this in the 'Mindful Mama' chapter.

A significant but often overlooked factor impacting your energy body is the energy of those around you and your environment. Atoms constantly emit and absorb energy, so it's important to be mindful of your company and safeguard your energy. Fortunately, I've discovered simple ways to positively affect your energy body; all it requires is your conscious awareness. In settings like the workplace, maintaining energy center health can be more challenging, yet it remains feasible with the right efforts. Whether you recognize it or not, you have undoubtedly experienced the energy of others.

For example, have you found yourself in a situation where you walked into a room and felt the heaviness of an argument or disagreement? You've thought, "Whew! You could cut the energy in here with a knife. It's so thick!" You didn't see the energy of the thoughts, words, and emotions in the room, but you felt their frequency as they lingered in the room.

I would also be mindful of the company you keep. Are you surrounding yourself with an upbeat person who inspires others and maintains a positive outlook? Or are you with someone who frequently complains, adopts a 'woe is me' attitude, and spreads gossip? These factors significantly impact your energy body.

The powerful Third Eye Chakra is located between the eyebrows, just above the bridge of the nose. Having a balanced and strong Third Eye is crucial when looking to conceive, and for your overall health, as the hypothalamus and pituitary gland, are a part of your

Endocrine System. Additionally, the nervous system significantly influences your thoughts and bodily responses.

Maintaining a healthy Third Eye is important not just for the physical functioning of your body but also greatly enhances your intuitive connection with your baby. This applies to telepathically communicating with your baby before conception, while in the womb, and once they are earthside. You possess the ability to connect with your baby on an energetic and emotional level, and this telepathic bond will promote an unbreakable relationship between you both. I will share exercises later that will help strengthen your Third Eye, allowing you to connect with your baby on a deeper level beyond the physical.

You can recognize when your Third Eye has become sluggish when you have scattered and confused thoughts. Yes, "mom brain" is real and certainly can contribute to this, hence why frequent Reiki is essential in supporting you. You may notice you're spacing out, becoming more judgmental and closed-minded, and even beginning to flake out on prior commitments. When I find myself experiencing this, I engage in a grounding meditation, which is shared in the next chapter.

Your seventh Chakra, the Crown, is located exactly by its name, the crown of your head. The Crown Chakra is the center that fuses body and spirit. It makes you feel one with all that is, the divine. It is the center of cosmic consciousness and enlightenment. The primary indicator of an imbalanced Crown Chakra is a feeling of disconnection from the divine or your higher self. If you're experiencing apathy or confusion and are questioning why conception isn't happening right away, this can upset your Crown Chakra. This is why it is essential to trust in Source and surrender during your pregnancy journey and in life.

Your Aura

Having explored the chakras and their functions, let's discuss your aura, which envelops your physical body and consists of seven distinct layers. Each layer serves a unique purpose, and your aura plays a role in safeguarding your physical body. Acting as a protective shield, it filters the energies you encounter before your chakras absorb them while also drawing in the positive energies you meet. Your aura is remarkably intuitive, understanding your needs without requiring your conscious effort.

Your aura changes for various reasons. It contracts and comes closer to your body when you're ill or stressed. Conversely, your aura expands if you feel healthy and vibrant or have just received a healing session like Reiki. Your aura usually extends a few feet around your body, but it can fill an entire room for those with an expansive, healthy aura. You may not realize it, but you have experienced someone's energy, particularly from those with a broad aura. These individuals don't need to say anything; their energy fills the room with confidence and positivity. You're energetically attracted to them like a moth to a flame and naturally want to absorb their energy, which your aura does. Therefore, using techniques to safeguard your energy is essential: you have limited energy to give and should steer clear of energy vampires.

The seven layers of the aura include the Etheric Body, Emotional Body, Mental Body, Astral Body, Etheric Template, Celestial Body, and Ketheric/Causal Body. These layers radiate outward from the physical body and correspond with the seven primary chakras. Each subsequent layer has a lower vibrational density as they move away from the body. Despite their outward expansion and differing vibrational densities, these layers maintain communication with one another. Reiki healing occurs within the Etheric Body, which is closely associated with the physical body. This layer is an energetic replica of your physical form and is vital for existence.

In Donna Eden's book "Energy Medicine" she states, "Your body cannot support life without its aura any more than the Earth could support life without her atmosphere."

Are you an Empath?

One of the most valuable insights I've gained about myself is that I am an empath. If you're not familiar, an empath is someone who feels emotions intensely, often absorbing the feelings and energy of those around them much more than usual. This deep capacity to feel others' emotions allows me to connect and empathize, which has been incredibly beneficial in my healing practice. However, I was initially unaware of the toll it took on me to carry others' emotions in my energy body. For years, I couldn't comprehend why I felt utterly drained after social interactions. I would enter gatherings feeling lively and sociable, yet as conversations progressed, I slowly became quiet, less engaged, and felt my energy fading. By the end of the night, I would hit a wall and feel completely exhausted. It wasn't until I met someone who inquired whether I was an empath that I started to understand. They asked me targeted questions, all of which resonated with me. These questions made me recognize the underlying cause of my fatigue after being around others: I was indeed an empath.

Everyone should safeguard their energy, but especially if you're an empath. Here are a few questions to help identify if you're an empath:

Do strangers confide in you right away, revealing intimate details of their lives? I've lost track of how often this occurs. Whether I'm in a checkout line, dining alone, or waiting to use a restroom, it happens. In every situation, people act as if we're long-time friends the moment they start sharing. What's intriguing is their immediate comfort with me that seems to effortlessly encourage their openness, often without them realizing it. This is a clear sign that you possess empathic qualities.

Do you sense and feel the emotions of others as they are your own? As if their pain or happiness becomes your pain and happiness?

Do crowds or busy places overwhelm you? Just as I shared, I would begin feeling vibrant and happy, but after spending some time in group settings, I began to feel drained and reserved.

Do you find that you require more time to recharge compared to others? As a mama, personal time can be scarce, but prioritize quiet moments for rejuvenation, particularly for empaths.

Understanding your energy body, whether you're an empath or not, is crucial during your pregnancy. People often unknowingly project their energy, concerns, fears, and emotional imprint birth stories onto you without realizing the impact of sharing these narratives. Their intentions are not malicious; they believe they are helping by preparing you for potential challenges. However, from an energetic standpoint, this can adversely affect your well-being, leading to unnecessary fear and anxiety. For those who already struggle with anxiety and intrusive thoughts, this can amplify every concern and hinder your ability to enjoy a healthy, vibrant pregnancy. Striving to maintain energetic balance, preserving your energy, and cleansing your energy can provide the extra support you need.

During my pregnancy, many people asked why I opted for an unmedicated birth at a birthing center. I was inundated with questions such as, "What if something goes wrong?" "How far is it to a hospital?" and "What happens if the pain becomes unbearable?" I adjusted my responses accordingly depending on the topic and who was asking questions. For instance, I responded with, "I know this may seem unconventional to you, but it feels right for my body and my baby." I acknowledged any reservations expressed by saying, "I understand your concerns; however, I've chosen a trusted team that I know will do what's best for my baby and me. If an urgent issue arises, they will ensure that I'm transferred to a hospital and cared for appropriately." If someone consistently projected their worry and anxiety, I established clear boundaries with them. I'd respond, "I appreciate your concerns, but this pregnancy and birth is a very energetic experience for me. I prefer to engage in conversations that uplift my spirit, keeping my mind and energy in the direction I want them to go." My husband was amazing at filtering these interactions, and when I wasn't up for responding, I relied on him to address the matter.

Due to my frequent self-Reiki, which helped my energy remain as balanced as possible, I typically addressed them with a clear mind, calmness, and confidence, drawing from my positive energy. However, there were moments when I was more reactive, my hormones got the best of me, or I had just grown tired of answering questions instead of feeling supported in my decision. I am only human, but in these few occurrences, I gave myself grace.

Gaining insight into my energy body and its influence on my physical body provided me clarity to enhance methods for preserving my energy. This adaptation has become indispensable to my daily life, especially during my pregnancy. Rather than isolating myself from high-energy environments or feeling perpetually drained, I now can self-regulate and avoid absorbing too much energy from others, and you can too. When I do inadvertently pick up energy from others,

I've learned effective ways to release it. Because of the impact understanding energy has had on my life, I am passionate about teaching others the significance of recognizing their energy body and its influence on their well-being.

Pregnancy is a special time in your life and one you may only experience once. Remember you are responsible for your energy body. Your child will attune to the frequency of your energy and the energy within your environment as early as when they are in utero and certainly once they are earthside.

As you've discovered, energy is all around you and heavily influences your physical body. Therefore, the key questions are: how can you maintain your energy, steer clear of energy vampires, and ensure your energy body remains intact and resonates at a high, healthy frequency? In the next chapter, let's discover techniques to help safeguard and cleanse your energy body so you and your child can live a more mindful and energetically aligned life.

CHAPTER 5

Energetic Responsibility

Throughout the years, I have embraced methods to manage my energy responsibly. The tools listed below have effectively preserved, safeguarded, and cleansed my energy. I incorporate these into my daily routine, sometimes using them several times based on the energy I am encountering or experiencing. I have also shared these with my clients, who have reported positive results. You can adapt these tools to fit your personal style. Please feel free to use my suggestions as a starting point and adjust them to meet your individual needs.

Safeguarding Your Energy

Circle of Prayer

I engage in this practice for myself and my family every day, both in the morning and at night before sleep. You can call on whatever Source you believe in; if prayer isn't your style, you might connect with your higher self. The point is to use what resonates or feels meaningful to you. This could include names like 'Father Sky, Mother Earth, God, Universe, Source, Guides, or Angels.'

"Father Sky, Mother Earth. I'm drawing a circle of divine loving energy around my spirit and my body. In this circle, I place the white light of peace, the blue light of healing, the red light of energy, the golden light of wisdom, and the pink light of love. In this circle, I am safeguarding my energy and only allowing what is for my highest and best to enter. Amen."

If I find myself in a situation where I neglected to say my circle of prayer beforehand and notice that I'm around someone whose energy doesn't align with mine, I mentally say, "Return to Sender." In cases where the other person is being rude or negative, I not only say, "Return to Sender," in my mind, but also send good energy back to them filled with love and light, as that's what they need most at that moment. Being consciously aware of my energy and theirs allows me to set a positive, energetic example even if they're unaware of my actions. It's important to remember that people can sense energy, even if they can't articulate it.

Energy Bubble

I picture a bubble of white light surrounding me to safeguard my energy. When I visualize it, it resembles a large bubble from a child's toy, and I feel perfectly placed inside it—safe and sound. The bubble is transparent with a hint of iridescent color, sparkling in the sunlight. If I encounter energy that doesn't resonate with mine, it softly rebounds off my bubble, returning to the other person. As I send the energy back, my bubble also transfers the love, light, and compassion they need, just as I mentioned above.

Grounding Visualization or Meditation

Even though this is a beautiful mindfulness technique, I feel it's essential to include it in this section because it helps support your energy body. I typically do this while brushing my teeth in the morning to prepare for the day, especially before going out in public. In the early stages, it may take you more time to run through it, and that's okay. When practiced ritually, it will become second nature. I encourage you to slow down and try the visualization as you read along. For a bonus benefit, perform this visualization while standing or sitting barefoot outside.

Get yourself in a comfortable seated position with your feet flat on the floor. Take some deep breaths, and in your mind's eye, see a bright white light swirling above your head. On your exhale, guide the light to the top of your head to your Crown Chakra. Stay here as long as you need to, taking in any sensations, colors, or visions you see. When you're ready, on your next exhalation, guide the white light to your Third Eye Chakra between your eyebrows, again pausing as long as you need. Next, direct this white light to your Throat Chakra, remaining mindful of anything coming up. Keeping with the rhythm of your breath, escort the white light to your Heart Chakra in the center of your chest. Continue to focus and breathe. Exhale; take the light to your Solar Plexus just below your ribcage, again bringing awareness to any bodily sensations. When it feels right, guide the light now to your Sacral Chakra just below your navel, staying present with anything arising during this time. On your next exhale, lead the light to your Root Chakra at the bottom of your tailbone. In your mind's eye, see the white light split into two and travel down each leg, over the thighs, knees, and shins, past the ankles, and to the bottom of each foot. Once the light arrives at the bottom of the feet, you begin to see tree roots growing from the bottom of your feet. Use your exhalation to guide the roots deeper, larger, and stronger down into Mother Earth. Sit with your roots connected into the earth for as long as you need. When you're ready, on your inhales, slowly begin retracting the roots back into the bottom of your feet.

I've performed this with open and closed eyes as a guided meditation. It helps ground my energy when I may not have had the opportunity to be outside yet and helps me feel secure and strong in my body. This is helpful from an energy perspective because when I encounter challenging or uncomfortable situations or people, my energy is solid and grounded, helping me face any obstacle.

As an energy worker, I particularly appreciated having this in my toolkit because it allows me to connect with my body and energy. When attending to clients, if I suddenly feel pain in my right knee, which wasn't present during my morning grounding visualization, it suggests that I am tapping into the pain my client is experiencing, or it represents an emotion they have stored in that area. As a mother, this practice will enhance your connection with your child beyond just the surface. To listen to this grounding meditation, visit www.melbraun.com.

Cleansing Your Energy and Space

Visualization

As you will discover in the 'Mindful Mama' chapter, visualization is a potent technique and one I've found extremely useful for my energy body. As an empath, I use this method daily when showering before bed. Even with my diligent practices, I can still pick up others' energy and when it's not a vibrational match, I need to discard it.

I let the water wash over me as I stand in the shower. I imagine the water washing away the day's troubles, observing it flow down the drain. I repeat in my mind or aloud, "I am cleansing away whatever is not serving me for my highest and best," along with anything else that feels relevant at that moment. If a specific situation comes to mind during this practice and/ or any negative emotions tied to the thought or situation, I will add that to my visualization and wash it away, too.

If I am out in public and find myself around someone who is not the right vibrational match for me, I will excuse myself to the restroom and perform this same ritual at the sink while washing my hands. If you're an energy worker, I highly suggest implementing this after every session to preserve your energy and not take others' energy home.

Another technique I use to cleanse my energy, especially after giving Reiki sessions to others, is a Japanese "dry bathing" method called Kenyoku. It's quick, effective, and easy to do.

Start by placing your right hand on your left shoulder and sweeping down your chest diagonally to your right hip. Then, place your left hand on your right shoulder and sweep diagonally to your left hip. Next, place your right hand on your left shoulder and brush down your left arm to your fingertips. Then, place your left hand on your right shoulder and brush down your right arm to your fingertips. To watch a quick tutorial on how to perform Kenyoku, visit www.melbraun.com.

Energetic Cords

Energetic cords attach to you from your partner, parents, friends, strangers, and especially your baby. If you're an empath, these cord connections are heightened due to your sensitivity. These cords transmit energy and emotions between two spirits. There are positive cords and ones that are not serving you and need to be severed. For example, when a baby grows inside the womb, an umbilical cord is formed to provide nutrients. Think of energetic cords as invisible umbilical cords with everyone you come in contact with; even eye contact matters. Some cords provide positive vibrational, energetic nutrients, while others deplete you. Those that deplete you are the ones that are usually found in toxic or dysfunctional relationships. Cords from these relationships need to be cut as they can make it challenging to interact healthfully or move on from said relationship. I've worked with clients whose cutting cords with certain family members was necessary. This act wouldn't disconnect their relationship. However, it would support them in interacting peacefully and not becoming entangled in the web of drama.

For those who have needed to cut cords with someone from a past relationship, it may take a few cord-cutting sessions before the cords are entirely severed. This is due to the emotional attachment of the person/ relationship. In these sessions, I've found my client verbally communicate they are ready to detach and let go, but their energy or subconscious tells me otherwise. When this happens, the cords cut will reform. A visual of this would be to think of a pesky weed you pulled in your flower bed, but the seeds from the weed remained. A week later, you notice the weed growing again because the surface weed was removed, but the seeds (the deep-rooted, attached emotions) lingered. More attention is needed to remove the weed from your flower bed entirely.

As for your loving relationship with your baby, this is a healthy, caring, positive, energetic cord. This invisible, intertwined thread keeps you energetically united, just as you were bonded physically when they were growing inside the womb. This is another way, as a mother, you can connect and communicate with your baby, which is helpful. On the flip side, there are scenarios where cords need to be severed from the mother and baby. An example would be if your baby continues to cry and you feel their anxiety. This is an unhealthy cord that needs to be cut. Suppose you're anxious because your baby is anxious. In that case, you cannot console your baby to the highest capacity as you would if you were detached from this low vibrational emotion. This is a time to cut the anxious cord to care for you and your baby.

Another example of a cord needing to be severed between a mother and baby would be if the mother feels a sense of loss that the baby is no longer physically connected to her. The emotion of grief associated with this feeling of loss can fester into larger problems that can create physical ailments, as you will learn more about in the following chapter.

I have benefited from cutting cords with my son to keep our energy among us harmonic, along with friends and family members, in my Reiki practice, and with strangers who have unconsciously attached cords to me. In my Reiki Master training, I teach how to sever these cords and other energetic techniques to support the energy body. If you're not trained in severing energy cords, I recommend seeking out a qualified professional to help you.

Cleansing Your Space

It's great to have good habits of cleansing your energy body, but that does you no good if your space is energetically heavy.

I had a woman reach out to me to do Reiki on her animals who had survived a house fire. During the session, she shared the upsetting details of the fire. She had left for work and shortly after received a call from her neighbor that her home was on fire. She rushed home, darted inside, and rescued her animals. All came out unscathed physically, but the emotional scars remained.

Even though the woman wanted the session for her dog that day, I quickly identified that she needed a session, too, so I worked on her dog and her simultaneously. She was angry about the fire and felt something she had worked so hard for had been ripped away. She was now living in an apartment and fighting with the insurance company on the claim. I realized not only was her anger lingering in her energy body, but it was also being projected into her space. Her animals also picked up on these emotions and took on this low vibrational energy. I also noticed some heavy energy from the previous tenant who had lived in the apartment before her that needed to be cleansed, too. She told me she cleansed her house when she first moved in but didn't even think to do it at the apartment she'd moved into. She had chalked her heavy and depressive emotions up to experiencing and dealing with the fire but didn't even give it thought that some of those emotions could be contributing to the previous tenant's energy remaining in her apartment.

After our session, she felt energetically lighter and noticed a positive mood boost in her dog's behavior. She did as I suggested and cleansed her apartment that evening. I followed up with her a few days later, and everyone's energy, including hers, was brighter. She was sold on the importance of routinely cleansing the energy in her space and planned to commit to it.

Being an empath, I am always sensitive to energy wherever I go and the energy in my home, but even those who are not empaths experience the impact of an energetically cleansed space.

Here are specific times you'll want to cleanse your space:

- If you've had vendors in your home performing work
- If guests were staying at your home

- If you've experienced the loss of someone or a job (This would also be a good time to set intentions while performing the cleansing. More on this below.)

- If you are going through a breakup or divorce

- If you or someone in your home has been under the weather

- Around the full moon as the moon's energy will additionally support releasing what is no longer serving you for your highest and best and allow you to make room for what you desire to attract in your life

- If you're feeling stuck in life

- Before you bring your new baby home

- And, of course, if you feel like your home needs a refresh

Energetically cleansing your space is not only for your home but also your workspace and certainly hotel rooms or Airbnbs while traveling. In Reiki II, I teach how to use certain Reiki symbols to cleanse a space, which is a great tool when traveling.

How to Cleanse Your Space

When cleansing your space, you want to neutralize the stagnant energy first. I like using Frankincense for this step when I perform house cleansings and cleanse my own home.

I light the frankincense and place it in an abalone shell, which keeps it secure as I walk around the rooms. Then, as I'm walking, I use a large feather to waft the gentle smoke to the perimeter and corners of each room. Energy likes to linger in the corners of the room like cobwebs, so when you're cleansing your space, you want your intention to be for the smoke to go to each corner as you go around the room. As I'm wafting the smoke, I say a prayer, whatever feels right in that moment. For example, you may say, "Father Sky, Mother Earth. I cleanse this space of all negativity and only allow what's for my and my family's highest and best to dwell here. Amen." After you have gone around the perimeter of the room, continue to waft the smoke as you walk through the center of the room. Take your time and be intentional as you go from room to room in the space you're cleansing.

After neutralizing the entire home or space you're cleansing, you can place the frankincense in a container or another shell and allow it to burn out completely.

Next, you'll want to refresh the space with something sweet. I like to use Myrrh for this step. You repeat the same steps as you did with the frankincense; however, I say another prayer while performing this step. Again, I say whatever feels right at that moment, but an example may be, "Father Sky, Mother Earth. I refresh this space with the sweet scent of Myrrh. May it be pleasing to you and only allow for positive, bright, and loving energy to dwell here. Amen." I then place the Myrrh in the same container as the frankincense and let them burn together.

An additional tip while cleansing your space is don't forget to cleanse your mirrors energetically. Mirrors hold energy and need to be cleansed, too.

I like to incorporate candles into my energetic cleansing practice. Each color represents a different intention. White is my go-to color for cleansing. It purifies you and the space and produces enlightenment and healing. Purple is for divination, power, and healing. Dark blue is for knowledge, focus, and truth, while light blue is for peace, patience, and creativity. Pink candles are for love, romance, and friendship; green is for prosperity and compassion and can also be used for love. Yellow is for communication, trust, and happiness. Orange is for self-confidence, optimism, and success. Combining the cleansing with candles of intention can add some extra magic.

Crystals can be another magical addition to your cleansing and your space in general. The secret to picking out the right crystal for you at that time is not to know what each one represents. When I go to a crystal shop, I let the crystal intuitively draw me in and hold it to see how it feels with my energy before reading about its properties. It's incredible how I'm instinctually drawn to one and read about it, and it's exactly what I needed to support me at that moment. I do, however, have a crystal for each chakra that I enjoy keeping around. At times I'm looking to incorporate an intention in cleansing my space; I like to make a crystal grid to magnify the intentional energy I am calling in.

- Clear Quartz connects with the Crown Chakra and is known as the "Master Healer" because it harmonizes all chakras. It aids in concentration, stimulates the immune system, and balances the body.

- Amethyst connects with the Third Eye and happens to be my birthstone. It opens your intuition and is a go-to for stress, fear, and anxiety relief, which is wonderful for a mom-to-be, can help with mood swings, and is associated with healthy cell regeneration.

- Kyanite is an excellent crystal for supporting your Throat Chakra. It can also help with communication, clear negativity, and clear blockages. It is excellent to have with you if you are around others who are negative or carrying baggage; it will keep your energy clear and their energy out. It is one of the rare crystals that do not require cleansing.

- Rose Quartz supports your Heart Chakra. This crystal is known for universal and unconditional love. It purifies and opens the heart to allow deep healing, love for self, and peace. It also enhances the bond between mother and baby during pregnancy and after birth.

- Citrine connects with your Solar Plexus and can activate creativity, enhance concentration and motivation, strengthen your intellect, and stimulate the brain. It can also release fear, depression, and phobias.

- Carnelian supports the Sacral Chakra and boosts confidence and courage. It can also help overcome abuse of any kind. It stimulates creativity and motivation. This crystal connects with the reproductive system, so it is the go-to for fertility and pregnancy and can help balance hormones.

- Tourmaline is an excellent crystal for grounding and safeguarding your energy. It connects with your Root Chakra, balances the yin and yang in the body, and enhances energy flow, which assists in removing blockages. Tourmaline is known as the "mental healer" because it balances the right and left hemispheres of the brain and changes negative energy to positive. It also offers protection against electromagnetic frequencies from electronic devices, such as cell phones and computers. I keep tourmaline under my bed mattress and the couch cushions, in my car, and I wear it when going out.

- Selenite is a power crystal that charges and cleanses all other crystals it comes in contact with and cleanses your space. It's a beautiful crystal for calming and instilling peace and supports you during meditation by helping you connect with God, guides, angels, and your higher self. If you have a sore or tight part of the body, try putting selenite on it for relief. This is a stone you do not want to get wet.

Your Child Feels

As you learned, your chakras take in energy and radiate it outward. Your energy is contagious, especially to your child.

I had only taken my son on two trips via airplane, and on the flight home, I had to travel alone with my son. At the time, he was nine months old and very active, so sitting in a confined space for a long time certainly posed its challenges. I made sure to wake up extra early so I wasn't rushed, but I became anxious after he wouldn't take his morning bottle, which was totally out of character. My mind started spiraling into the details of what could go wrong from his hunger while traveling. "Would he cry non-stop from hunger, or would he finally eat?" "Am I going to be 'that mom' who disrupts the entire plane?"

While washing his bottles so they were all fresh for travel, he was getting irritable and ready for his morning nap. I hurriedly finished, packed the clean bottles, and loaded our bags into the car. My son fell asleep quickly, and as I was saying my circle of prayer while driving to the airport, I took some deep breaths to calm the anxiety I had created. I told myself I would be relaxed and confident while traveling home, and all would be well. Once arriving at the rental car return, my son was still fast asleep; that's when I received the notification our flight was delayed. I first huffed and started to feel uneasy again, then thought, "Maybe this happened for a reason so he can have more time to nap?" My son slept about 45 minutes and was ready to go.

As we made our way into the airport, I had the diaper bag on my back, my son in the car seat in the stroller as I pushed him along, his backpack of bottles, toys, and blankets in the bottom of the stroller, and I was pulling our suitcase with the travel crib strategically placed on top. We were loaded down, to say the least.

As I approached the desk to check our bags and the car seat, I noticed a man coming up behind me to check his bag. I turned around and said, "You can go ahead. It's going to take me a moment." He responded with, "Wow, you've got quite the load! Looks like you've done this a time or two." Me laughing, "Ha! This is my first time traveling alone with my son." "Well, you'd never know it," he smiled as he checked his bag.

At that moment, I realized I was exuding the calmness and confidence I had coached myself on just an hour prior; even this stranger felt it. We experienced another delay in our flight's takeoff time, and I didn't let it ruffle me. My son was the calmest he'd ever been on that flight, and I have no doubt it was due to me remaining calm and confident in the uncertain situation.

Cleanse your child, especially after traveling.

We had taken our son on his first long flight to the West Coast for a wedding. Not knowing what to expect with a 5.5-hour flight and 3-hour time difference, I planned to expect the unexpected. He did phenomenal on the flight there, adjusted to the time change with ease, and did even better on the flight home.

Once we landed and deplaned, my husband waited for our luggage while I changed him into a fresh diaper and pajamas so that we could give him another bottle and put him to bed as soon as we arrived home. We assumed he would be a little tired the next day with all the excitement and stimulation from the wedding and needing to catch up on extra sleep.

The next day posed some challenges. He was a little fussy, which was out of character for him, but we expected some adjusting back to our normal routine of sleep and feedings. He didn't have much of an appetite, which led me to become concerned about him becoming dehydrated due to the 100-degree days we were having. Because of the heat and his having never experienced it before, my logical thought was maybe he was like me, and when it was crazy hot, he didn't want as much to eat either. I talked myself through every scenario to explain the unusual behavior I could think of. The nights, however, came with more of a shock.

He was waking up three to four times a night, not just crying but with a high-pitched scream as if he was in pain. I went through the usual motions; maybe he was hungry, so I gave him a bottle. The next waking with shrills, I gave him tummy calm thinking maybe his stomach was upset from the travel. I even rocked him to sleep because that was the only solution. I knew he was in another big developmental phase per the app I used to track these stages, but he seemed extra clingy and needed much more comfort than usual. Something just felt "off."

After three nights of not sleeping, I felt like we had regressed back to the newborn stage of being up every two hours. I was on a call with a Reiki friend, telling her what was going on and the first question she asked was, "Did you clear your and his energy when you got back?" I felt like such a dunce. It had totally slipped my mind this time.

That afternoon, in between naps, as we played in his room, I energetically cleansed myself, him, his room, and our house. I found a few cords while scanning his body that I removed as well.

I let him lead on when he needed to nap for the remainder of the day and for how long. It was a later bedtime than usual, but we went through our usual nighttime routine. I was still concerned he hadn't eaten enough during the day, so I was fully prepared to be woken throughout the night due to him being hungry.

I woke up a little after 6 am from hearing him on the baby monitor. He had slept through the night. That day, he played and ate as usual, and he and his schedule were back to normal. I knew in my gut the energy we cleared had been the culprit of his major upsets. Who knows how long we would've remained in that cycle if I hadn't cleansed him and our space.

Even though this is my expertise, I am human too and, at times, need to remember to utilize these tools. I'm grateful for others around me who are also energetically aware and responsible for reminding me of the power of energy from time to time. What a gift.

CHAPTER 6

The Emotional Body

Newton's third law, that for every action, there is an equal and opposite reaction, plays a significant role in the emotional body. For every emotional thought you have and experience (the action), you are signaling to your body how to respond (the reaction) to that thought. We are said to have over 400 emotional experiences each day. You're constantly being inundated with emotion, and when not dealt with healthily, it's just a matter of time before these emotions show up physically in your body.

So, how do we understand more about the emotional body and how these emotions manifest physically? Before continuing, I want to say I'm not discounting Western medicine. I do believe there is a time and place for medicine and surgeries. However, I have seen in my practice that when we focus on the root cause, the emotional element as to why one may be experiencing what they are, many of these ailments that once troubled them dissipate on their own. I am sharing what I've witnessed in hopes of bridging the gap between Eastern ideas and Western medicine, as I feel there is room for both, ridding ourselves of the Band-Aid approach and beginning to heal from within.

Envision yourself preparing to go on a hike. You get dressed in sweat-wicking clothes and put on a hat and hiking boots. You load up your backpack with nutritious snacks to sustain you while you're out, along with a few other essentials and water. You make your way to the trailhead and take in the sights. You're surrounded by mesas and red rocks towering around you as the sunshine illuminates each rock's perfection. Walking along a crushed rock pathway, you notice different-sized rocks scattered along and around the trail. Each rock you become aware of represents an emotion you've encountered, and the path now represents your life's journey. Some rocks are more prominent, showing the characteristics of the heavier emotions you've faced in your life, such as loss, grief, intense anger, and overcoming abuse. The smaller rocks along the path signify the feelings you've felt that have had a lesser impact on you that were a minor upset.

As you walk past each rock, the ones that resonate with a memory associated with the particular emotion, you stop to pick it up and place it in your pocket. Some rocks capture your attention, and others you breeze past them, not giving one thought that rock needs to be picked up. These are the emotions you processed quickly when they happened and are not taking up space in your body.

As you continue down the path collecting certain rocks, your pockets become full, so you start to harbor them in the backpack you're wearing. As you continue along, you now become uncomfortable with the weight of the rocks you're carrying, but you continue to soldier on. Once you run out of room in your backpack, you place the smaller rocks in your hiking boots. With nowhere else to carry the additional rocks you're collecting, you now begin to hold them in your hands, eventually carrying countless rocks in your arms. What happens as you continue along the emotional rock path and choose not to process your feelings? You become weighed down by the rocks, and finally, the weight of the rocks outweighs your physical body's weight. Ultimately, you become so weighed down that you can no longer move forward on your hike, enjoying the breathtaking scenery you once took in. All of your attention is now on the weight of the rocks, the emotions you're carrying, which have become too heavy to transport any further. This is when I see clients in crisis mode.

Psychosomatic is derived from the Greek words psyche, the mind, and soma, the body, meaning mind-body related. Psychosomatic disorders occur when mental factors create physical symptoms in the body where there is no detectable physical illness. Because of this, a plethora of physical problems arise in the body from our thoughts, emotions, and beliefs. We've been conditioned to believe the mind, body, and spirit are separate entities, but they are intrinsically connected. As an energy practitioner, this clicked for me immediately and was the only thing that made logical sense of what I had experienced in my life and my Reiki practice. I believe most, if not all, diseases and physical disruptions in the body are psychosomatic. We become our thoughts.

Countless clients have come to me for Reiki sessions with unexplainable ailments. They've seen every professional known to man, received innumerable tests and scans, and still come up empty-handed on an answer or solution to what they were experiencing and why. Feeling defeated, frustrated, and at a dead end, they would be led to me for Reiki.

Unsurprisingly, in their sessions, we uncovered through their energy bodies that the unprocessed emotions they've picked up and carried throughout their lives have now created physical disruptions in their bodies. These disruptions serve to bring their attention to what they have been emotionally avoiding. When we peel back the layers, these troubles didn't begin overnight. Their body had given plenty of signs along the path, signaling it was time to process, but they continued to push through, collecting more rocks along the path without lightening their emotional load of previous encounters.

Every thought, emotion, and experience make an energetic impact on the physical body. The body has memory, and when there is a negative connotation, this creates tension in the body, adversely disrupting every system. For example, those who suffer from chronic stress or anxiety will usually experience digestion issues. This is due to our bodies being wired for a state of survival. If you're busy digesting and eliminating, you cannot run away from the predator chasing you. As a result of this state of stress you're in, your nervous system detracts from the 'rest and digest' state and stays in the 'fight or flight'.

As you learned in the Energy Body chapter, your chakras store emotions. When emotional upsets, long-term stress, overwhelming occurrences, and emotional imprints are repressed, they create imbalances in the body. These imbalances disrupt the flow of chi (your energy) through your body, making this movement of energy sluggish. This is when you experience the ailment that has now captured your attention. Reiki is an excellent modality, as it brings balance and harmony to your energy body, which, in turn, brings balance to your emotional body. You can avoid unnecessary physical ailments by continuing to maintain energetic alignment.

In Chinese Medicine, it is said that unprocessed emotions impact particular organs. Let's delve into specific emotions and what organs they affect.

Grief, depression, and loss affect the lungs and large intestines. In my practice, I have found clients who have experienced deep, unprocessed grief suffer from breathing problems. One client, in particular, hadn't smoked a day in her life and grew up in a smoke-free home but found herself diagnosed with lung cancer. There was no history of cancer in her family; she was the first. When giving her a distant Reiki session, I could feel the immense grief and loss she was harboring. She confirmed she had experienced a significant amount of loss throughout her life and hadn't processed any of it. Medically, there was no understanding of how she ended up with lung cancer. It seemed clear that what I felt in her energy body was the culprit.

The emotions of anger, rage, and resentment show up energetically in the liver and gallbladder. I personally experienced the side effects of pent-up anger. In my early twenties, I began having unexplainable stomach pains. I would wake up multiple times throughout the night, and it became hard to eat as everything seemed to upset my stomach. I went to the doctor and received multiple scans with still no real answers. I became desperate for relief and agreed to have my gallbladder removed, as the doctor believed it was the cause of my issues. Mind you, I had no gallstones, didn't eat fried foods, and was not overweight, all the main contributors to needing your gallbladder removed. Even after having the surgery, I still experienced pain. Even though my physical gallbladder had been taken out, the energy of it remained along with the repressed emotions.

It wasn't until I began receiving energy work that I experienced relief. During my sessions, I would have emotional releases, realizing I had been carrying emotional imprints experienced from my childhood my entire life. My repressing this anger, guilt, and shame had heavily affected my Solar Plexus, the center of raw emotions and where my gallbladder resided. During these sessions, I realized I was on a path to healing from within and embraced the tears and involuntary movements as my body unwound. I surrendered and let my subconscious mind and body dance together in a processing revolution. Still, to this day, I no longer have any pain. I wish I had known then what I know now about how repressed emotions affect the physical body. From a Reik perspective, anger is poison to the body. I wish I had exhausted all holistic options first. I would still have a gallbladder and one less surgery. I hope sharing my story helps you or someone you know to explore other avenues before committing to surgery. Yes, at times, surgery may be necessary, however, avoiding unnecessary surgeries allows you to avoid physical distress, which has its own energetic consequences.

Clients, who hardly drink, have come to see me with elevated liver numbers and not understanding how this happened. Once working with them, we uncover hidden anger or resentment. With an open mind and heart and a few sessions, their numbers regulate. They have the bloodwork to prove it.

From a Reiki standpoint, worry is the second poison for the body. Worry and nervousness affect the spleen and stomach. The spleen is a small but mighty organ whose primary function is to filter your blood. It is also responsible for your immune system, so clients I've worked with who are continually getting sick are the ones who frequently worry, even if they don't consciously realize it. They may not know they worry so much until we discuss it. I have found that these clients strive to control everything, continuously living in the future and neglecting the present. If you struggle with remaining present, incorporate the tools in the following chapter for support.

From a chi viewpoint, weight control becomes an issue when the spleen and stomach have an energy deficiency. Strengthening the spleen's energy optimizes your body's ability to digest food efficiently. Also, when we tend to be worried, we look for comfort, which usually resides in overeating. This can also lead to excess weight gain.

An exercise that you may find helpful is talking to your body and listening for the answer. For example, if you suffer from unexplainable stomach issues, ask yourself, 'What am I not digesting in my life?' and see what comes up for you. Reiki can be a great way to bring awareness to your emotional body, which, in turn, supports you physically. I have also found it's caused me to be more empathetic and compassionate to others, as it allows me to see them from a different perspective. Those who showed to be very angry were often hurting deep down inside and used anger as a defense mechanism because they didn't feel safe.

When we encounter fear or face the unknown, our mind assesses it by interpreting similar past experiences that made us uncomfortable. Our primitive brain is still wired for survival, so the unknown of our essential needs being met, like food and shelter, and whether a predator is going to eat us, is engrained in our psyche. When your survival needs are stable, your brain can overanalyze all the 'what if' scenarios. The fear of change and everything that could go wrong creates kidney imbalances. I've seen this show up for clients with chronic lower back pain, adrenal fatigue (your adrenal glands are located on top of the kidneys), and habitual kidney stones.

You may be wondering what releasing repressed emotions looks like in a session. Once I connect with my client's energy body, I work with my 'clairsentient' intuition. I then feel sensations in my body that mirror what my client is feeling. I am not taking on their energy or ailment; it's simply a way of communication.

For example, I can feel when a client is on the verge of having an emotional release because my eyes will fill with tears as I empathically connect with my client. I can feel if a client is suffering from anxiety because I will begin to feel my chest getting tight, as this is what anxiety feels like to me. While administering Reiki, once I feel relief, I'll check in with my client to see how they feel. They, too, notice relief.

If you don't feel ready to work with someone else to help process your emotional body, you can lean on interoception to guide you and take it a step further with a technique I call 'Body Talk.' Interoception is a practice that brings awareness to what we are witnessing and the environment we feel inside us. To take this concept deeper, I converse with my body to get to the cause of a disruption or discomfort. I do this through meditation. As I'll share in the next chapter, meditation is simply about being present, and one of my favorite ways to meditate is walking. Here's a story of how I communicated with my body, and I was shocked by what it told me.

Body Talk

Upon confirming my pregnancy, my symptoms became clearer. The surging hormones, tearful reactions to random things, and the overwhelming fatigue were no joke. I tried to explain these feelings to my husband, and he empathized the best he could, but I still felt like I was lost at sea. The unrelenting need for daily naps was both draining and frustrating, conflicting with my ambitious plans for my business. Balancing my mental drive with physical limitations became a daily struggle, often leading to tears of frustration. Despite understanding the importance of nurturing new life within me, the constant battle between mind and body left me feeling defeated.

When I was ten weeks pregnant, I woke up one morning with a cyst on my left ankle. It seemed to have appeared overnight. I hadn't done anything different for it to appear and certainly hadn't injured it to cause inflammation there. During this time, I barely had enough energy to maintain a gentle yoga practice. While it didn't impede my ability to walk, I constantly felt discomfort.

The cyst persisted, and by day 5, I started to ponder why it was there and what I had done. During a walking meditation that day, I felt the need to communicate with my body. I was accustomed to dialoguing with my body when health issues arose and was genuinely surprised I hadn't considered this earlier. I had been too preoccupied with my 'poor me' mindset due to fatigue; negativity had begun to dominate my daily life.

At this moment, I thanked my higher self and body for the reminder to reconnect. I told my body that I was listening. I then drew my attention to my left ankle and asked my body what it was trying to tell me and why this cyst had developed and wouldn't leave. I couldn't believe what I heard. "You are not fully stepping into the femininity of this pregnancy. You must cherish this beautiful time in your life; it is a gift. You're exerting too much energy and living in your masculine energy. You cannot do what you're used to doing right now, and that's okay. Give yourself grace and embrace this time in your life."

Something about this moment and message flooded my body with comfort and peace. My body was correct. I was having internal conflict with the changes my body was going through and showing resistance to this "new me" without even realizing it.

At that moment, I had a conversation with my body out loud. While walking, I thanked my body for all that it was doing for me and this sweet life I was growing. I thanked it for being strong and healthy and was grateful this baby had a safe womb in which to prosper. I made a solid promise that in the future, instead of resisting the nap I needed, I would welcome it.

A few days went by with this new routine. Interestingly, I felt lighter and less tired than the weeks before and felt like I had settled into my pregnancy and the new way of life. I was in a harmonic flow with myself and my daily routines, and it felt amazing. I felt so wonderful that I had forgotten all about the cyst that had popped up out of nowhere on my left ankle. I had forgotten about it because it was now gone.

This was a reminder that we are capable of so much. We can be our own medicine when we slow down and truly listen. Our body knows the exact prescription.

I constantly educate clients about how our bodies always communicate with us; we just have to listen. When an illness or discomfort of some sort arises in the body, it is a sign of an imbalance, and in my case, it was psycho-emotional. This was a perfect example of me living in an old version of my life that was not serving the new version. I was so fixated on keeping up with everything I was used to doing that I wasn't living in sync with my body and the season it was in. Once I stopped resisting and began embracing the positive changes that were happening within me and around me, everything about my pregnancy started to fall into place.

This may seem like an outlandish story if you're new to communicating with your body, but I highly encourage you to try it. You will undoubtedly be amazed at what your body says to you. In this example, my walking meditation showed me gratitude for everything my body was doing right for me: growing a healthy life inside of me. This experience altered my entire attitude and mindset and allowed me to flow with ease through pregnancy.

You will inevitably experience peaks and valleys throughout pregnancy and motherhood. When you experience the valleys, take the time to reflect and show gratitude for all the things that have gone and are going right. Think about the previous valleys you've overcome, the learning opportunities that came with them, and how this situation will prove no different. If we constantly lived on the peak, we would take them for granted. It's our nature. The valleys humble us. Pregnancy is no different. Yes, there will be hard days that may even lead up to weeks, but remember, you're in the valley. You will go back up to the peak. The valley is only temporary.

I also want to point out that everyone's level of interoception, which is your innate ability to sense and interpret your internal bodily sensations, differs depending on what they have experienced. These experiences, such as emotional imprints, shape one's internal world. I'll share more on this later; even what a child experiences in utero plays a factor. Interoception is a continuum as one goes through life and will evolve as one encounters new occurrences. Because of this, remember some can handle a saucer-sized amount of stress, others a plate, and some a platter. No one's experience or internal world is inferior to the other; it's based on perception and what that person can handle.

The same goes for your child. If you can manage a plate or platter of stress but your child is more emotionally sensitive, a saucer size may be all they can handle. Recognizing this allows you to be conscious of how to support them on an emotional and energetic level so their physical body remains balanced and nurtured innovatively. Your primary focus is to make your child feel safe, as this is integral to all aspects of their life.

When bringing my son home from the birthing center, the original plan was to have him sleep in the bassinet beside me. Instead, bed-sharing felt appropriate for us and made it much easier for me to breastfeed throughout the night, allowing me to get more sleep. Many disapproved of this idea, providing reasons why they felt it was unsafe. However, we took all precautions to ensure his safety while co-sleeping, such as ensuring he slept on his back and was free from encountering any blankets or pillows. The idea of epigenetics played a role in us choosing to bed-share. In my mind, my son had spent almost ten months growing inside the comfort of my womb. Now, being exposed to an unknown environment outside of the womb, it was my job to make him feel as safe as possible, nurturing his needs. As others expressed their concerns and how difficult it would be to transition him from our bed to his crib, I begged to differ. My logic was that if I catered to his needs early on, he would understand he was safe, and whenever he needed me, I would nurture him. This would make the transition to the crib even more manageable because of this emotionally established relationship.

At 4.5 months, we hired a sleep coach to provide additional tips on the transition. I was mentally prepared for the tough nights ahead, especially the first one, as the sleep coach informed me it could take up to two hours for him to self-soothe to sleep. When beginning the first night, I filled the room with Reiki and gave my son Reiki. As I shushed and patted his bottom, the Reiki allowed me to remain calm and centered, and my son fell asleep in under 45 minutes. The sleep coach was amazed he fell asleep on his own so quickly, especially because of our bed-sharing. For me, it made total sense. I had met his needs since day one, and he trusted I would continue to do so.

Epigenetics

Scientific research shows how a child's experiences and environmental influences affect the expression of their genes. This emerging area of science is called epigenetics, and it shows that nature vs. nurture is no longer a debate. Both are an integral part of one's makeup.

Children inherit DNA that makes up their genes from their biological parents, such as their height, hair color, and temperament. Chemical marks in the DNA regulate how much of a particular gene is expressed. The compilation of these chemical marks is known as the 'epigenome,' and the experiences a child has reposition those chemical marks and the information they transmit.

The epigenome can be affected by positive and negative influences, relationships, and encounters. Each experience leaves an imprint on the gene, swaying the chemistry of a gene's expression. All of these factors play a role in the architecture of a child's life. This begins as early as a child in utero and continues into the early stages of life when the brain is rapidly developing. What seems like a minute experience at the time can lead to impressions that last a lifetime. As shared above, these impressions can affect organ systems, create poor physical and mental health, and affect the child's behavior. This is why a safe and healthy emotional and physical environment is crucial to a child's development impacting how they show up as their future self and to others as they mature.

We collectively heal generational emotional imprints by investigating and revealing the emotional body. These imprints relate not only to cultural, economic, and familial distress but also to the emotional burdens transmitted through our DNA from one generation to the next.

Consequently, your grandmother influenced your DNA while your mother was in utero because that is when her eggs were forming.

Focusing on healing your emotional imprints will help block their transference to your child. For example, say you were a victim of sexual abuse as a child, which, as an adult, makes you distrust others and leaves you shut down to romanticism and a healthy, loving relationship. When this emotional imprint is left unprocessed, you may notice that your child as a young adult expresses these same behaviors even though they did not physically experience the abuse. The emotional imprint from your experience was passed down to them, keeping you and your child in old, unserving patterns. I believe this is also why there can be a history of medical issues in a family. Since emotions affect our DNA, health issues will continue until the emotional imprint is released. I share more on this topic in the 'Baby Communication' chapter.

Once I understood the magnitude of this, I decided the buck stopped with me. I was no longer allowing these imprints to dictate my life. I did not want to experience the same unnecessary hardships my family had encountered, and once I knew I could change the narrative, I committed to doing so. Now, becoming a mother, this is even more meaningful. My son was born with a cleaner slate and will not have to carry the imprints I did. Our bodies want to heal themselves. It's our duty to create the space it needs in a non-judgmental way, so they can do what they were designed to do.

Rituals

When the season of spring rolls around, we feel the itch to come out of hibernation mode from the winter months and focus on spring cleaning. I think of rituals in the same light. Rituals are a spring cleaning of our soul, a way to process repressed emotions, a cleansing and releasing of whatever is no longer serving us for our highest and best self. A ritual is another technique you may want to lean on if you'd like to begin releasing bottled-up emotions on your own. It is another go-to for me.

I incorporate rituals in many seasons of my life. When I'm feeling energetically or emotionally heavy, when I'm looking to call something in, such as an opportunity or as a way of energy and emotional hygiene. I've realized through my practice I do not have to be consciously aware of what needs to be processed at that moment; my subconscious will step in and do the work for me.

I describe our emotional body as a five-gallon bucket. When our bucket is full and overflowing with emotions, there's no room to attract what we want. We must process, release, and make room for the positives we desire. Each ritual will create room in your bucket, allowing you to fill the new-found space with high vibrational emotions.

A ritual is a sequence of actions or activities performed ceremoniously. The ritual I love connecting to the most is working with the energy of the full moon. Have you ever been to the beach during a full moon and noticed the tides are more extreme? This is due to the moon's gravitational pull. Our bodies are comprised of over 60% water, so I believe during the full moon, the same tides, our emotions stir up within us. Do you notice you're more emotional around the full moon? If you've never paid attention, try it and see what comes up. People have repeatedly reported how a full moon affects their mood and sleep, and you can ask anyone who works in labor and delivery that an abundance of babies are born around a full moon. This can't be coincidental.

During my full moon ritual, I cleanse my space and energy body and use specific affirmations and prayers depending on the moon's energy that month. The Native Americans named each full moon to keep track of the seasons. Each of those seasons brings different supportive energy during that time.

For example, the Wolf Moon is the first full moon of the calendar year, which is a time of reflective energy from the previous year and a time to clarify and define our goals and intentions for the new year. I always give gratitude for the lessons and abundance from the previous year, release what I do not want to bring into the new year, and focus on elements that will serve my passion for the present year. Wolves are known as pack animals, so you may notice that you have the desire to deepen relationships with others or yourself during this time.

During my rituals, I spend time meditating and journaling. I write down insights I gain from my meditation or explore the emotions I am experiencing at that moment. If any emotions arise while journaling that no longer serve me, I fold the papers that contain my thoughts, feelings, and words and safely burn them in a fireproof container. This act symbolizes my release to the Universe. Burning the paper represents purification, transformation, and closure. It could signify letting go of limiting beliefs, releasing a letter to someone who has affected me emotionally, and forgiving them, or breaking a habit I want to change. Whatever comes up is unique to me and that specific moment in time.

I have also incorporated Reiki into my ceremonies to add support, especially if what I'm releasing feels heavy. For example, if I release anger from a situation that occurred, I will give Reiki to myself over my liver and my heart if that feels right. Now that there is an energetic space there, I will fill it with the loving, healing energy of Reiki.

The intention of a ritual can be a powerful way to support your energy body. For a free guided meditation and full moon ceremony to release whatever is no longer serving you for your highest and best, you may visit www.melbraun.com to participate in an interactive ritual.

The quote by Ghandi, "Be the change you wish to see in the world," resonates deeply when talking to your emotional body. When you do the work to process stored emotions from your encounters, and those passed down, you create a brighter future for the next generation, which is something to be proud of. It takes bravery to discover and face what makes us uncomfortable, but once we come out on the other side, we are reminded of how powerful we are in mind, body, and spirit.

CHAPTER 7

Mindful Mama

Do you believe in magic? I do and have witnessed magical experiences in my own life and the lives of others. Once you understand that you're a master magician of your own life, you will realize that you have the power to create your reality. You must commit to directing your brain in your desired direction. How can you take control of your mind instead of letting it control you?

Intrusive thoughts can feel like your worst enemy and begin occupying the free space in your mind. Your mental responses are influenced by what's been stored in your emotional body, which often consists of negative thoughts arising from your upbringing or emotionally scarring experiences. While it may require considerable effort to rewire your thinking patterns, the first step toward change is to become an observer of your thoughts.

I experienced this firsthand when I learned I was pregnant. My husband and I attended our first ultrasound, where we saw only a sac, no baby, but they confirmed I was indeed pregnant. Two weeks later, I had a follow-up appointment to check on the tiny embryo. Typically, I'm not anxious, but genuine fear gripped me as I worried we might receive discouraging news at the follow-up. I found myself replaying this scenario repeatedly in my mind, like a film. Once I realized what

I was mentally rehearsing, I stopped. Instead of criticizing myself for these troubling thoughts, I gave myself grace. Still, I wondered where these disturbing thoughts originated from.

After taking a few deep breaths, I recognized that I was both ecstatic about the possibility of us having a baby and grappling with feelings of fear and loss. I understood it was natural to feel apprehensive about the changes ahead, yet I reminded myself that I often appreciated change in my life, as it offered opportunities for personal growth and fresh perspectives.

Once I identified the source of my thoughts, I reassured myself that my feelings were completely normal. I acknowledged these intrusive thoughts as mere thoughts and released them. I knew how influential my thoughts could be in shaping my reality, so I consciously directed my energy toward the feelings I desired for myself and my baby. At that moment, I began to visualize my baby developing in the womb. As I cradled my abdomen, I communicated to my baby that they were safe, expressing my excitement to be their mother and the deep love I already felt for them.

Two weeks later, we attended our check-up and heard our baby's strong heartbeat at 145 bpm. Happy tears flowed down my cheeks as my husband and I held hands. We even spotted the tiny peanut developing in the sack where my womb was nurturing them.

Keep in mind that wherever we focus our attention, our energy, and consequently, our mind, follows. Being mindful and selective about your thoughts is crucial. For instance, if I ask you to avoid thinking about a pink elephant, what comes to mind? That's right, a pink elephant. Instead of fixating on undesirable situations or outcomes, intentionally shift your thoughts toward what you wish to achieve.

Your thoughts shape your reality, so what strategies can you adopt to steer your mindset in your desired direction?

Mental Rehearsal

Neuroscientists, those who work to understand the nervous system, which includes the brain, have discovered that when we mentally rehearse something, it activates the same neural pathways that light up when you are performing the task in real-time. Therefore, mental rehearsal gives you the confidence to face challenging situations, which, for the premise of this book, prepares you for pregnancy and birth, but these fundamental tools can be applied to all aspects of your life. By consistently applying positive mental rehearsals, your stress and anxiety levels are reduced because you have repeatedly rehearsed your desired outcome.

Mental rehearsal can start as soon as you decide you want to conceive. I began visualizing my ideal birth experience during my first trimester, continually imagining every detail. I pictured myself calm and confident in the warm, relaxing water of the birthing pool, trusting my body to handle the contractions as they came. I envisioned connecting with my breath, feeling lighthearted, strong, and excited to meet my son as I held him in my arms for the first time. I repeatedly envisioned myself reaching down to assist in delivering him. I am proud to say these mental rehearsals made me feel prepared and empowered, allowing me to give birth without any fear. I have no doubt they can have the same effect on you, regardless of your chosen birth method. Initially, I was unsure of what to expect when giving birth for the first time, but the videos my doula had recorded of me in labor demonstrated to me first-hand how everything I had rehearsed came to be as I brought life into this world.

While this book centers on energy and mindfulness, I want to emphasize the significance of physical movement during pregnancy and how it can contribute to your mental rehearsal practice.

When I became pregnant, my desire to support both myself and my son grew stronger. While I was already a Certified 200-hour Yoga Teacher Trainer, I aimed to deepen my knowledge of prenatal care. Consequently, I enrolled in a certification program to become a Registered Pre- and Postnatal Yoga Teacher.

Throughout this training, I found it captivating to discover the changes occurring both in my son developing within me and in my own body during this time. To help you appreciate the wonder of both you and your baby, I will share a few intriguing insights about the stages of pregnancy in this book.

A significant portion of the prenatal yoga teacher training focused on practicing safe and supportive prenatal postures and effectively teaching them to others. I participated in these classes and incorporated the techniques into my yoga routines. Throughout this time, I supported my body with therapeutic movements and worked on aligning my breath with each asana, yoga pose. This training enabled me to harmonize my mind, breath, and body, which was invaluable during labor. I would mentally and physically prepare by rehearsing specific poses, slowing my practice down, closing my eyes, and envisioning myself in the pool, relaxing between contractions. When labor began, I effortlessly slipped into a meditative state, allowing my body to take the lead. After extensive rehearsals, everything unfolded smoothly and confidently during labor, just as I had envisioned and prepared for.

Intentional Power Board

When I used to host an online monthly membership where we gathered throughout the month to learn new educational topics, a guided meditation, and a monthly full moon ceremony, one of my favorite activities was in December. We would each create our own Intentional Power Boards in preparation for the New Year. Each member crafted their board to visually represent what they were calling into their life, constantly reminding themselves of what they desired to accomplish or receive. Many psychological studies have demonstrated the effectiveness of this technique. After every member completed their board, we would gather for our Zoom chat, and each of us would present our power boards, sharing the items we intentionally chose to live on our board, the significance of each carefully selected image or quote, and what we were calling in for the upcoming year. It was fascinating to reconvene the following year and recap what came true on our boards.

My board not only featured intentional aspirations, but I also included photos of what I was already grateful for, which fostered a sense of abundance. Among these was a family photo of me, my husband, our dog, and the supportive community of people connected to my business who provided financial, energetic, and emotional support.

If envisioning your ideal pregnancy and birth feels difficult, I suggest making an intentional power board to map out your desired outcome. Once you've assembled your board and reflected on it, close your eyes. Allow yourself to fully experience the emotions of the items on your board manifesting. Engage all your senses, and then express gratitude for the dreams depicted on your board becoming a reality.

When combining the visualization technique with the senses, your brain can hardly tell the difference between this being a feeling you have conjured up or if it is your reality.

According to cognitive science, consistently mentally rehearsing your desires or keeping your intentional power board nearby helps keep your goals in focus.

Uncertainty breeds fear, triggering cortisol release. Known as the stress hormone, long-term exposure to cortisol can lead to multiple health problems, such as a weakened immune system, high blood pressure, anxiety, and depression, to name a few. Positive mental rehearsals, on the other hand, aid in diminishing the fear of the unknown. Paired with gratitude, they boost oxytocin, also known as the love or bonding hormone, to counter this stress response. So, the more you guide your brain to gratitude, trust, and love, the less your body will live in the stressed fight-or-flight mode, the primitive part of our brain wired for survival.

Why is mental rehearsal combined with gratitude important in pregnancy and birth? Cortisol slows down your body's labor progress, so this delay can affect your body's natural response to go into labor. On the other hand, oxytocin is responsible for contractions that assist in thinning and dilating your cervix, guiding your baby down the birth canal. The more oxytocin you have, the more expedited your labor can be. An expeditious and happy labor and delivery experience is something I think we can all agree we want to occur, and mental rehearsal can be a crucial factor in making it your reality.

Intentional Affirmations

You can teach an old dog new tricks; neuroplasticity, formed through repetitive motion or thought, shows this. Even though you cannot erase the neural pathways already developed, your brain is malleable and constantly influenced by external factors. You can rewire your brain to steer it toward the outcome you desire. This is done by repeating a new positive thought with the aspired emotion you want to feel over and over so it becomes a more energy-efficient pathway for your brain to travel. This can be done through intentional affirmations.

As you've learned, everything is energy, and each word spoken carries its own frequency. Studies have shown how negative words affect water droplets. The negative words make the water look distorted; however, the positive words turn the water into patterns of beautiful snowflakes, each positive word casting its unique piece of art. Because of this phenomenon of the power of frequency each word carries, speaking your intentional affirmation aloud carries a higher resonance.

How do you choose the proper intentional affirmation for you?

For example, if there is a negative recurring thought you have, such as, "It was hard for my mother to get pregnant, so I'm sure it will be the same way for me," it's not the thought you need to rewire; it's the belief that it will be difficult to get pregnant that you need to reframe in your mind. So, in this example, an intentional affirmation may be, "I am grateful for this body. I trust my body and believe I will get pregnant with ease and surrender to the divine timing of my baby's soul choosing me as their mother. I am healthy, I am strong, I am vibrant."

Now, let's add the emotion associated with this intention. Think about how it will feel to see a positive pregnancy test. Create the visceral response in your body. Feel the joy, the wholeness you're adding to your family, and even the jitters of stepping into motherhood. It makes the array of emotions that may overcome you more real when what you've been so deeply wanting is coming true.

Whenever the negative recurring thought creeps in, replace that thought with your intentional affirmation. It's up to you how you perform this affirmation, whether thinking in your mind, journaling or speaking it out loud. From an energetic perspective, as you just learned above, I highly suggest speaking it out loud. Positive words, like gratitude, emit a high vibrational frequency, positively affecting your energy field. By speaking your intentional affirmation out loud, you're driving your mindset toward your desired direction and supporting your energy body. This is where your true power lies. You're now becoming a vortex of positivity, and this is how the law of attraction works. Not only are you thinking, feeling, and visualizing what you want, but you're now attracting that exact vibrational match in your external world. This is how you become pure magic.

Now that you understand how the law of attraction works, how do you deal with the adversity of intrusive thoughts or outside distractions from others that can infringe on your positive mindset?

Step one: Become aware of whether you're inflicting these thoughts or if they are coming from an outside source.

Step Two: If these thoughts come from you, regroup and follow the above actions. Acknowledge the thought, let it go, and replace the negative narrative with positive mental rehearsal and intentional affirmations. I would suggest having a list available with applicable affirmations, so you're always ready to combat the negative with the positive at a moment's notice.

Step Three: Be gentle with yourself if you notice you're the one inflicting these thoughts. The idea of mental rehearsal and intentional affirmations may be new and will take practice. As Yoga Sutra 1 says in "The Yoga Sutras of Patanjali" book, "Without practice, nothing can be achieved."

Step Four: If you realize an outsider is invoking these toxic thoughts, ask yourself, "Was there a situation they went through that is making them project their fear onto me?" "How can I communicate to them how this affects me and what I am striving to accomplish by keeping a positive mindset?"

As I mentioned in the 'Your Energy Body' chapter, others will unconsciously project their fears onto you, and I shared ways to have a productive conversation if these occurrences should arise for you. Your primary focus during conception, pregnancy, and the postpartum period is to safeguard your energy and mental headspace, which, as you've learned, go hand-in-hand.

Meditation

Mindfulness techniques are crucial for staying focused on the present moment, and meditation is an excellent tool to help you develop mindfulness. The act of meditation brings awareness to your thoughts and your emotional state, along with what may be going on in your physical body. When practicing a mindfulness technique such as meditation, you are directing your attention to what is happening in the now. Fear stems from the uncertain future; fear and anxiety fade by being present. Your strength lies in embracing the now.

Somewhere along the way, people have been led to believe that you must be a monk, sitting in a lotus position, to meditate. This is completely false, and if you're new to meditation or don't know how to meditate, I will show you the simplicity of it, and once committed to it, you too will experience its tremendous benefits. The frequency in which you meditate supersedes the duration, so make it a priority to meditate multiple times a week, a little bit every day is even better.

Simply put, meditation is about being present in whatever you're doing. You can meditate while you're gardening, walking, cleaning, or in a relaxing position. Let's break each of these examples down and explain their benefits.

If you're choosing gardening as your meditation, be present on how the dirt feels on your hands; take in the vibrant color of the flower you're planting and maybe even its fresh, sweet scent. If you're going for a walking meditation, notice how the strike of your foot feels on the surface you're walking on. Listen to the birds sing, feel the wind gently blow across your face and through your hair, and smell the fresh air. Let's say you're washing dishes; how does the warm water feel on your hands? Notice how satisfied you feel that you were able to make such a delicious meal that nourished your body. And my favorite, the relaxing position. Here, I focus on each breath's natural rise and fall, completely quieting my mind. For a soothing guided meditation that serves as an introduction or is useful for a quick reset, visit www.melbraun.com and enjoy it for free.

Breathwork

We can learn a lot from watching a baby breathe. They instinctively practice diaphragmatic breathing, engaging the diaphragm, the muscle under the lungs, with each deep breath. Each inhale through their nose expands their belly as oxygen fills their lungs. On the exhalation, their belly begins to fall and contract slowly. Instead of the term' sleep like a baby, ' we should really say 'breath like a baby,' as there are marvelous benefits.

When we feel stressed, our breath becomes shallow. This creates physical tension in the body as it activates the sympathetic nervous system, putting us in fight-or-flight mode. Shallow breathing has adverse side effects, such as weakening our immune system and making us more fatigued. If we already struggle with anxiety, shallow breathing can trigger panic attacks, keeping us in a negative mindset.

Being mindful of your breath and activating breathwork, such as Ujjay breathing, offers wonderful benefits. The Ujjay breath, also known as the victorious breath or ocean breathing, is performed by inhaling through your nose while keeping your mouth closed, simultaneously creating space in the back of your throat as you breathe deep into the belly, feeling your diaphragm expand. Keep your mouth closed and your jaw relaxed as you exhale through the nose, preserving the space in the back of the throat. As you exhale, notice your breath becoming audible, resembling the sound of ocean waves, which is how it got the name "Ocean Breathing."

This breathing technique is used in yoga and not only supports the supply of extra oxygen to your muscles as you flow through the asanas but also offers excellent health benefits. The Ujjay breath stimulates the Vagus Nerve, the heart of the parasympathetic nervous system, activating the signal to get your body in a state of rest and digestion. This diaphragmatic breathing has been shown to lower blood pressure, relax muscles, de-stress, and improve cognitive function. This breathwork can also harness your intuition, which we will dive into later in this book.

We can survive days without water and longer without food, but we cannot survive without breath. As you read along, let's do a quick exercise incorporating the Ujjay breath. Take a moment to get into a comfortable position, whether this be sitting in a chair with your feet flat on the floor and your hands relaxed in your lap or lying down. Take a few moments to breathe in the natural rise and fall of the breath and quickly scan how you're feeling. Do you feel stressed, tired, or notice any discomfort in your body? Now, focus your eyes on something that isn't moving, like a wall or object. Keep your eyes open, and begin the Ujjay breath, inhaling and exhaling as slowly as possible. There's no rush. All that matters in this moment is each breath. Solely chase the breath, not your thoughts.

When it feels appropriate, pause the Ujjay breath and reconnect with your natural breathing rhythm. Reflect on how you feel now compared to when you started. Remember, your breath is always there as a home base to return to.

Introducing children to breathwork from a young age equips them with the skills to manage stressful situations. This is a powerful tool that can serve them throughout their lives. I also recommend practicing alongside them to set a positive example. I believe there's no such thing as starting too early with breathwork and mindfulness; the benefits are invaluable.

The Power of Gratitude

Positive Psychology focuses on positive thoughts and behaviors, which we've discussed above. Expressing gratitude releases dopamine and serotonin, the two neurotransmitters responsible for our emotions. These chemicals not only make us feel good, but they can also improve sleep, mood, and immunity.

At some point, we began to take our health and bodies for granted. Conversations with those who have fought incurable diseases highlight this reality. Good health and bodily function have transformed from blessings into mere expectations. Rather than appreciating everything our bodies do well, we often dwell on what's going wrong, grumbling over every discomfort—especially during pregnancy. We replace moments of gratitude with feelings of anger, frustration, and disappointment regarding our body's issues, overlooking all the positive aspects of our health. Cultivating gratitude serves as a powerful remedy for both mind and body, as they exist in interconnected harmony.

Journaling

Another one of my favorite mindfulness techniques to help me remain in the present moment is journaling. It's proven beneficial for me on many fronts.

The first way it has helped me is by slowing down and clearing my mind. Although I'm a proponent of therapy, journaling is accessible any time, with pages always prepared to listen; all you need to do is grab a pen and begin writing. I prefer the traditional pen-to-paper method, but if you are more tech-savvy and would prefer typing out your journal entries, the act of doing it is more important than the method.

Journaling also helps me become more present with my thoughts and emotions. When something is troubling me, I can process those emotions, preventing them from becoming stagnant and stored in my body in unwarranted ways as you learned in the 'Your Energy Body' chapter. This also applies to recognizing the origins of my intrusive thoughts, allowing me to become an observer of them rather than letting them dictate my reality. Additionally, I use journaling to clarify my goals and intentions, especially when I am unsure about a particular idea or situation.

I also enjoy journaling about various events going on in my life. You can explore relevant topics or address current challenges, which are enjoyable to revisit later and recognize life's victories. This practice allows me to reflect on how I've overcome hardships that seemed impossible to tackle. These entries remind me that I can face challenges; often, what seemed tough was simply a new situation I needed to learn how to navigate.

I journaled throughout my pregnancy to connect with my son while he was in the womb. I will go into more depth about this and my experience in the chapter 'Baby Communication.' However, it is a special gift that I can refer to those journals at any time, relive my pregnancy all over again, and one day give to my son to keep.

Mindful Movement

Yoga is a wonderful way to nurture yourself during pregnancy. As I mentioned earlier, practicing yoga while linking my breath to the postures not only aided me physically during labor but also served as a form of moving meditation, with the connection between breath and each asana being essential. By concentrating on your breath during movement, your mind cannot dwell on anything else, allowing you to fully inhabit the present moment. For instance, whenever I step onto the mat, my physical practice mirrors my internal state. If I usually excel in a specific pose but struggle that day, it directly reflects my current mindset. I encourage you to discover a mindful movement practice that benefits you both physically and mentally.

Disconnect

In today's tech-driven world, it's essential to take time to unplug. Nature provides the ideal remedy to escape the chaos. It always offers just what you need in the moment. Forest bathing and grounding are two of my preferred methods for disconnecting, and the best part is that they cost nothing.

Forest Bathing

The Japanese expression shinrin-yoku translates to 'forest bathing'. This term emerged in the 1980s when there was a tech-boom burn-out, and many Japanese civilians worked up to 80-hours a week. The physiological and psychological exercise of forest bathing invited them to disconnect from their busy lives and commitments and reconnect with nature. Many health benefits have been shown from spending time in nature. Due to it reducing the stress hormone cortisol, forest bathing reduces stress and anxiety, and boosts your immune system, all things that are excellent to support you in your pregnancy and thereafter. If you can't spend time outdoors, consider bringing nature indoors with potted plants to elevate your décor and your mood. Adding a selection of rocks, crystals, or seashells can enhance the effect. Lastly, simply opening the windows in your home to welcome fresh air in will connect you with nature.

Grounding

Grounding has become a widely discussed term and practice within the wellness community, but what does it mean, and how does it work?

Grounding involves connecting with conductive surfaces, allowing your body to draw the Earth's energy. You can achieve this by sitting, standing, lying, or walking on grass, sand, dirt, or plain concrete. Research has shown that grounding can lower blood pressure and cortisol levels at night, leading to improved sleep. It also enhances mental clarity, elevates mood, reduces inflammation, and promotes calmness.

Silence

In my Reiki practice, I have found that many clients fear silence and struggle with it. They've become addicted to chaos to avoid what might arise in moments of stillness. One of my favorite ways to embrace silence is while driving, and I've encouraged my clients to try it, too. Personally, I find it a meditative experience, helping me remain aware of my surroundings while also fostering a sense of calm. During my time in real estate, when faced with difficult transactions, I always leaned on quiet moments to find resolution. This approach consistently worked for me, allowing me to devise effective solutions and successfully close deals.

Also, while driving in silence, I've had some of my most profound thoughts and creative ideas propelling my business forward. If you're searching for an answer to a personal ongoing question or a resolution in a challenging situation, turn to silence and be open to receiving what comes through. You may surprise yourself.

Reiki

Reiki serves as a powerful mindfulness tool, enabling you to disconnect from the external environment and refocus on your inner self. In the chapter on 'Reiki and the Physical Body,' you discovered how Reiki helps your body enter a parasympathetic state, often referred to as rest and digest, which is essential for promoting a positive mindset. When your body releases the stress hormone cortisol, it reverts to survival mode, hindering your progress toward your goals. Make it a point to incorporate Reiki whenever possible to keep your mind aligned with your desires.

The 10-Minute Rule

Once I became a mother, I remember asking my husband what I used to do with my time before this phase of life. Time management plays a significant role in your mindset and is a juggling act. It can pose challenges when time doesn't seem to be on your side when caring for a little one or multiple children.

I was having a catch-up conversation on the phone with a friend who is a mother of three and is expecting her fourth. She told me about her recent volunteer work, her kids' extracurricular activities, and now all the summer fun they were having. It was her last summer with them as a family of five, so she admitted she was going a little overboard with commitments to savor this time together before their new addition.

At this point in our conversation, we were vulnerable about how hard it is to juggle being a present mom and wife, tending to things around the house, working, trying to slip in time for ourselves, and managing everything else life decided to throw our way.

She said her husband was at his breaking point with the house, and she admitted rightfully so. Their bedroom had become their second laundry room; clean clothes in a pile, ready to wear, and the only place in the house where her husband had his own space, his office, had become the catch-all room. Not to mention their dream outdoor patio renovations had gone south, and their roof had leaked in multiple areas of their home, so blowers and construction materials were everywhere, the workers continuing to come in and out of their home to complete the project that of course experienced multiple delays. Their home, which should bring them comfort and solitude, was a constant tornado of chores, and it was taking its toll on their mental health.

I talked about my yard work and how much I missed spending time outdoors. However, my time was now quite limited, and weeds were overtaking the beautiful flowers I had planted. That's when a light bulb went off in my head. "You know what? Let's devote 10 minutes each day to tackle the essential tasks. We can do this before the kids wake up, during nap time, while they play outside, or after they go to bed. We can manage anything for just 10 minutes," I said enthusiastically.

Before my son woke up the following day, I walked outside with my weed bucket, set a 10-minute timer on my phone, and got to work pulling the weeds that had become my nemesis. I spoke kindly to my plants blooming amongst the chaos of weeds; I took in the fresh air and listened to the birds sing as I watched the sun slowly rise over the tree line. Before I knew it, my timer went off, and I pulled two buckets full of weeds out of my flower bed. I noticed how productive I felt and how peaceful and grounded I was starting my day in nature.

My flower beds were weed-free in six days, and I felt mega-accomplished. What had originally seemed like a daunting task became manageable. I decided to adopt this method with other tasks that needed my attention around my house and started breaking up the intimidating list of daily chores into bite-sized pieces. This freed my mind of constantly thinking about the long list of what needed to be tended to, making the items approachable and overall more productive because it eliminated the feeling of being overwhelmed.

The 10-minute method can be applied to anything. You could use this idea to get your workouts in, sprinkling 10-minute increments throughout the day, equating to 30 or more minutes daily, and maybe even beginning your day with 10 minutes of gentle yoga to wake up your mind and body. Perhaps you use this towards your self-care, spending 10 minutes journaling, taking an Epsom salt bath, meditating, or whatever measure you'd like to use to decompress.

R.E.S.T

During a walking meditation late in my pregnancy, I experienced a mix of emotions. I felt excited to be one day closer to meeting my son and exhausted from my growing belly, which was making restful sleep difficult. Also, the fear that my husband might miss the birth continued to creep in.

During this walk, I embraced a new concept I called the R.E.S.T method to aid myself in this phase: Recognize, Evaluate, Stillness, and Treatment.

The initial step involved recognizing and understanding my feelings. I observed I was feeling quite tired and uncomfortable as I had a little waddle while I walked. I also noticed I felt extra emotional, and the fear I felt was certainly a contributor.

Once I brought my awareness inward and recognized how I was feeling, I then moved to the evaluation step. Was my exhaustion due to a poor night's sleep, a sense of defeat from the physical changes I couldn't control, or simply feeling off from cosmic influences? (Like the Supermoon that intensified my emotions during the final weeks of my pregnancy, adding to the challenge of managing my pregnancy hormones.)

After reflecting on my feelings following my walk, I settled down in stillness and silence to meditate. I requested guidance from my higher self and my Spirit Team to reveal the solution that could bring me the peace and tranquility I sought. During this meditation, I realized I needed to express my emotions through writing. Not only would this help me process the emotions I was feeling, but sharing this vulnerable experience would also resonate with many others as part of this book.

After my meditation, I followed the clear instructions I was given. Instead of reaching for my favorite pen and journal, I grabbed my laptop. Cozied up on my couch, wrapped up in a blanket as my dog, Lily, gently cuddled beside me as she rested her head on my very pregnant belly, I began to write. What I wrote at that moment is shared in 'The Butterfly Effect' chapter. I hope as you read that section of what I was experiencing the final few weeks makes you feel seen and heard and is a reminder you're not alone.

The R.E.S.T method can be applied to all facets of your life and is not exclusive to pregnancy and motherhood. I hope embracing this principle brings you awareness and provides you with an action plan, guiding your thoughts toward your goals.

CHAPTER 8

Preparing to Conceive

You've now discovered how your energy and emotional body, along with your mindset, greatly impact your overall well-being. This is particularly true when you're preparing to conceive.

Unfortunately, conception doesn't always come right away for those who desire to be mothers. Some of my most cherished stories from Reiki clients are from women ready to conceive. In my practice, I've incorporated Reiki, visualization techniques, journaling, and whatever I intuitively feel the client needs to support her energy body to encourage conception. In the two stories I'm sharing, both women had very different backgrounds and life experiences that brought them to me for Reiki, but both desired to be mothers.

Before sharing these lady's stories, please consider that it might be sensitive if you've experienced a miscarriage. Ultimately, the choice to read it or skip it is yours. Should you choose to read, I hope their bravery in sharing their journeys offers comfort and hope, encouraging you to grieve and heal your emotional scars through Reiki and other therapeutic approaches, allowing you to find the relief you deserve.

5%

I met Sherry before I fully engaged with Reiki. I coached at a nearby Pilates studio where she frequently attended classes, so when I got my Reiki certification, she quickly became one of my first clients. Although she wasn't very familiar with Reiki, her holistic lifestyle made her eager to explore new modalities.

For nearly two years, Sherry sought Reiki sessions from me intermittently to alleviate her stress and anxiety. Though she already had a daughter, she felt that adding another child would complete their family. After experiencing one miscarriage prior to having her daughter, Sherry and her husband anticipated another smooth pregnancy, as their previous experience had been quite uncomplicated.

In one of our sessions, she opened up about her quest to conceive again. During their efforts to expand their family, they experienced an upsetting miscarriage, and a DNC was necessary for their situation. Following the procedure, they had to wait several months before attempting pregnancy again to allow Sherry's body to recuperate. When the fetal tissue was tested after the DNC, doctors identified a chromosomal abnormality, prompting rigorous testing for both her and her husband.

Tests revealed that her husband had a translocation involving one chromosome detaching and attaching to another. The specific break he had could lead to miscarriages in otherwise healthy pregnancies. The doctor mentioned that considering their stage in the process, their ages (both in their late 30s), Sherry's ovarian reserve, and her husband's translocation, their likelihood of conceiving, even through IVF, was 5%.

After visiting the infertility specialist's office, Sherry's husband felt discouraged and settled on the idea that they were only going to have one child. Sherry quickly remained optimistic and told her husband she heard there was a 5% chance and remembered her friend who battled ovarian cancer telling her, "You're a statistic of one. Don't let anyone else tell you what your story is."

A few months later, they decided to pursue IVF. They felt that seeking medical help for conception was essential for a healthy, full-term pregnancy because of her limited egg count. Their $15,000 out-of-pocket expense resulted in another heartbreaking disappointment. She allowed external distractions and the doctor's insistence on urgency, coupled with concerns about her low ovarian reserve, to influence her mindset. At that moment, Sherry recognized that she was pushing for pregnancy rather than trusting the process and leaning on her faith.

This marked a pivotal moment in her journey. She dedicated herself to maintaining her physical health and strength while emphasizing mindfulness practices, including positive mental rehearsals and intentional affirmations. Coincidentally, this was when I received my Reiki certification.

Sherry, while open to exploring other modalities, was skeptical of Reiki being able to help her but had reached a point in her conception journey where she felt like she had nothing to lose. Our established relationship from the Pilates studio gave her the confidence to try a Reiki session with me.

Unaware of her hardships, during our first session, I intuitively revealed emotions stored in her body, specifically around her uterus. My findings left Sherry a little shaken but open to exploring Reiki further. In our sessions, we worked on releasing the emotional imprints of anger and unworthiness attached to the multiple DNCs she'd endured. Sherry then committed to Reiki with me once a month. Within a few sessions, she was feeling more at peace and ready to surrender to the outcome of whatever was meant to be. I knew at that moment Reiki had brought her chi back into balance.

The day before turning 41, she discovered she was pregnant. Although she was accustomed to positive pregnancy tests, her past experiences kept her from feeling excited when she saw the plus sign on the stick.

About two weeks later, she contracted COVID-19. Due to her pregnancy, her body had shut down to protect it, which landed her in the hospital. During her time there, fear ensued, and her once positive mental rehearsals reverted to the negative patterns that had taken over her headspace in the past. "This is surely going to end the pregnancy." "I'm not worthy of this." "The doctor was right. This isn't going to happen." "This one's just like all the others," played repeatedly in her mind.

Upon leaving the hospital, she was about seven weeks pregnant and faced heavy bleeding, severe cramps, and passed material. She had grown numb to both the miscarriage process and the emotions linked to it, as she had endured nine devastating miscarriages at this point. The thought of sitting in the waiting room again among expectant mothers hearing their babies' heartbeats, and she wouldn't, was unbearable for her. The pain of it all was too much, so she chose to skip the doctor's visits and continued the daily motions of her life.

About a month later, it's Labor Day weekend, and she begins to feel extremely fatigued, prompting her to make an appointment with her primary care doctor before leaving town. They required her to take a pregnancy test, which came back positive. Nonchalantly and detached from emotions, she blankly told the doctor there was no way she could be pregnant and explained what had happened a few weeks prior, which was just like all the other miscarriages she had had in the past.

The doctor then performed a cervical check and said that the lining of her uterus seemed to be thickening, which indicated that she might be pregnant. Unfortunately, since it was right before the holiday weekend, the ultrasound tech was out of town, so an ultrasound couldn't be performed until the following Tuesday. The idea that she could potentially be pregnant began to sink in, but the worry of having COVID-19, along with all the medications she took, made her fearful of the outcome.

It was time for her appointment on Tuesday, and she told her husband to stay home. Again, she had been down this road before and didn't want to drag him through the mud with her. They began the ultrasound, and there it was—the sound of her baby's heartbeat playing on the monitor. Sherry was pregnant and about eleven weeks along, which was the same duration as the prior pregnancy that required the DNC.

Remaining optimistic but still jaded, Sherry went on to have bloodwork performed to make sure the baby didn't have the translocation. When she came in for her next Reiki session, I could feel her energy was different since I last saw her. I knew she was pregnant, which she confirmed and told me everything she had been going through. I asked her if she wanted to know what sex I thought the baby was, and she said yes. I picked up a strong presence of testosterone and believed it was a boy. I told her this soul had been with her before, and he told me he was ready and needed her.

The bloodwork came back, and Sherry was preparing herself for the worst. As she read the report, every potential abnormality showed "Negative." Tears rolled down her face as she continued to scroll, searching for something wrong, but there wasn't. Finally, Sherry was carrying a healthy baby.

Months went by, and Sherry religiously came in for her sessions, each time deepening her connection with the baby finally growing inside of her. Reiki helped support her, keeping her calm and putting her in a positive mindset versus one of fear.

At seven months pregnant, she was hospitalized due to uterine window, which is a complication of a previous cesarean section, where the uterine wall begins to thin. She was continually monitored for the next two months. Throughout this period, Sherry relied on Reiki for encouragement, so we resumed our sessions via distant Reiki while she was on bedrest in the hospital. Sherry faced not only bedrest but also the hospital's strict COVID-19 restrictions, which limited her family's visitation and intensified her feelings of isolation.

On March 12th, 2022, Sherry gave birth to a beautiful, healthy boy. Her and her husband's dream of adding to their family was finally complete. Even though her story was not exactly as planned, she used Reiki and mindfulness to control what she could, leading to a less taxing and stressful situation.

I believe that our working together released the emotional imprints left in her body from the prior miscarriages. Since her energy was balanced, it created more harmony in her home and in her husband's energy, which allowed for conception and for her son to feel safe in the womb and stay. Energy is contagious, and if your energy body is in a balanced, calmer state, others will feel it, too, including the embryo and fetus.

Sherry has become one of Reiki's biggest advocates. She has not only sent countless referrals my way but also went on to learn Reiki from me. Her original focus was to support herself and her family solely with Reiki. Still, after repeatedly experiencing its power, she is now starting her own practice, and I couldn't be prouder of her.

She'll be back

I have worked with multiple clients through their grief of miscarriage, but Lynn's story is one I will never forget.

During one of her routine Reiki sessions, Lynn expressed her desire to prepare her body for conception. I intuitively detected that her gut health was imbalanced and encouraged her to see a naturopathic doctor. After seeing the doctor and running some tests, the intuitive Reiki proved correct. She began restoring her gut health and taking proper supplements to return her body to a healthier state. Now, it was my job to continue to focus on her energy body.

In our regular catch-up before her session, Lynn revealed that she was expecting. Normally, I can immediately sense when a client is pregnant, but with her, I didn't feel that usual connection. Her pregnancy was very early, around six weeks, but she had a positive test result. Overwhelmed with joy, I shed a few tears and embraced her, knowing her deep desire to become a mother.

As we began her session, I connected with her baby in the womb and asked her to do the same. Souls communicate energetically, including babies developing in the womb. Typically, they are open to communicating with me telepathically in some fashion, but every soul is different. When working with expectant mothers, I communicate with the baby, introducing myself as 'Auntie Mel,' and describe how Reiki may make them feel, how beneficial it is for their development, and how it connects them deeper to their mama.

A week later, Lynn reached out to tell me she had been bleeding heavily and was going to the doctor. My intuition knew what was happening, but I consoled her the best I knew how and told her I was there to support her however she needed. She told me she would let me know what the doctor said. Unfortunately, not hearing from her was all the confirmation I needed.

When Lynn came in for her next Reiki session, she told me she had miscarried. We cried and hugged as she shared the news with me. During that session, I worked with her energy body to process and release the grief from this loss, and at that time, I heard what the sex of the baby was that she had just lost. I asked her if she wanted to know, and she said yes. "It was a girl," I replied. "I knew it," she responded through tears. "Her soul wasn't quite ready, but don't worry, she's coming back," I said with a soft smile and a few tears trickling down my face.

I had just finished my self-paced online Reiki I training module when she expressed interest in learning Reiki. Now would be a perfect time for her to learn and practice daily Reiki while I was on maternity leave. Additionally, I strongly believe everyone should learn Reiki I, as it focuses on self-healing, which is beneficial to all. She immediately enrolled and completed the course quickly. I continued to work with Lynn leading up to my maternity leave and we remained in contact even when I wasn't seeing clients.

After returning from maternity leave, we arranged a distant Reiki session. We took a moment to catch up, and I sensed her energy had shifted. "I'm pregnant!" she exclaimed with excitement. "Yay! I knew it!" I responded enthusiastically, raising my hands in the air, cheering.

"If I've done the math right, my due date is the same as the day your son was born!" She said. This sent chills throughout my entire body. "That's wild!" I replied.

This session exposed some repressed familial anger that needed to be released to calm her energy body. I offered suggestions on how she could capitalize on releasing these stored emotions during the full moon that week, as she would be additionally supported energetically during that time.

About a month later, we had another session, and Lynn's energy felt more collected. She told me she had taken the liberty to do what I had recommended and felt at peace with the once-angry familial situation. Her energy read that way, but something new tugged at me while working on her. There now was an unconscious fear she'd lose this baby, too. While working on her sacral chakra, her baby communicated with me and said, "Tell her I'm here to stay." I told Lynn what I heard and that there was no need to worry; this soul was sticking with her, but her baby craved to connect with her more. I encouraged her to start talking to her baby, which was only a sac, but its soul was very much alive. She confirmed she would. I told her I felt masculine energy and thought it was a boy. If it wasn't a boy, it was a girl with a strong personality. She was happy with either sex.

My favorite session during her pregnancy was the third one. We started with our usual catch-up, where she expressed how tired and nauseous she felt. Despite the physical challenges of the first trimester, her energy body seemed positive. I noticed she appeared calmer, and she had started communicating with her baby.

As I was working on her sacral chakra, the energy I felt from the last time had shifted. "Okay, I said it was potentially a boy last time, but I was wrong. I'm feeling a lot of feminine energy now. I think it's a girl," I said as Lynn smiled. "Do you have a name picked out? I'm hearing the name 'Rose.'" Her jaw dropped. Startled yet laughing, she responded, "Are you serious right now?" "Yes. I distinctly heard that the name 'Rose' is important," I replied. Lynn shared, "My husband's family is from El Salvador, and he had a special bond with his grandmother. When she passed, it was super hard for him. Because our families speak both English and Spanish, we need a name that translates the same in both languages. Mila is what we landed on, and to honor his grandmother whose name was 'Rosa,' if it's a girl, her middle name will be 'Rosa or Rose.'"

The hair stood on my arms and the back of my neck. I showed her the best I could through my laptop camera via Zoom, my arms covered in goosebumps. For me, this was total confirmation that it was a girl. "Well, I've got to tell you, this may be grandma reincarnated because this little girl is definitely feisty!" I said while laughing from the energy I felt. "That sounds about right," she responded. "His grandma was a strong lady and walked around town carrying a gun on her hip - she was feisty!"

Lynn was going for her gender test that week but would wait to share the results with her family for a gender reveal party. I followed up about two weeks later, impatiently waiting for the results. Lynn mentioned they were having the gender reveal party that weekend and promised to inform me of the results.

My phone buzzed with a text message. It was from Lynn. She sent a video and a text saying, "You were right!" I watched the video, which showed her hitting a golf ball, shattering pink powder everywhere. Tears rolled down my face as I watched her and her husband embrace each other excitedly while their family cheered in the background. Mila Rose was here to stay.

I worked with Lynn throughout her pregnancy. We concentrated on positive mental rehearsals and intentional affirmations and, of course, provided plenty of Reiki for both her and Mila. On September 18th, 2024, Mila Rose was born healthy and brings so much joy to her family.

These ladies didn't let a chapter dictate their story. Often, the challenges we face shine light on other positive elements in our lives, such as the incredible partner or support system we have by our side. When you intentionally channel your efforts positively, your mind, and your body will follow. Let's explore fundamental tools that will give you the confidence to surrender to the process and divine timing, just as these remarkable women did.

Reiki

In earlier chapters about the energy body and emotional body, you gained a comprehensive understanding of their crucial roles in your physical well-being. If you are preparing to conceive or are already pregnant, now is an ideal time to begin nurturing these two. As mentioned in the 'Why Reiki' chapter, my clients who faced challenges with conception discovered that Reiki helped identify underlying issues linked to trapped emotional imprints, leading to imbalances within their bodies. Once these emotions were released, their energy body regained balance, providing a welcoming environment for their baby's soul. The spirit of a baby is brilliant, and some may hesitate to enter a body burdened with generational imprints, as their soul's purpose is often to experience something different to aid their evolution. I also want to emphasize that experiencing a miscarriage depletes your chi (energy) similarly to childbirth, so consider using Reiki for replenishment.

By clearing the emotional obstacles affecting their energy body, clients elevated their vibration to align with the soul seeking to join their family. If you are struggling with infertility, I highly encourage you to explore Reiki as a viable option. I speak from what my clients have experienced, and everyone who committed to a regular Reiki practice successfully attained their goal of becoming a mother.

Remember, when your energy is balanced, it expands your aura, reverberating into your environment. Your external environment then mirrors your internal bliss. Everything within and around you remains in a calmer state of being. I believe this was the epitome of Sherry's ability to conceive, experience a full-term pregnancy, and give birth to a healthy baby boy.

You have also explored the intricacies of Reiki, engaging directly with your endocrine system. This modality facilitates optimal energy flow, ensuring balance within these systems. By maintaining hormonal balance, you create an ideal physical environment for conception. Additionally, you learned the negative effects of cortisol and how it infiltrates your system, impacting almost every organ and tissue in the body. Frequent Reiki will help reduce stress and anxiety, factors that can hinder timely conception.

Intentional Power Board

When you're ready to conceive, apply the ideologies learned from the 'Mindful Mama' chapter to conception. Keeping your intentional power board as your visual representation of what you desire will allow these principles to stay at the forefront of your mind and drive your energy toward the outcome you want.

There are various ways to create your intentional power board. I like to make my board on material I can have out and around my house so I can look at it daily. I've used a corkboard, poster board, and collage picture boards. Maybe you're more tech-focused and choose to make your board via an online platform like Pinterest or Canva. Perhaps you want to blend both options and make your board on material, then take a picture of it and save it in your photos on your phone to refer to throughout the day or place it as a screen saver on your desktop. However you choose to incorporate the board is up to you. The act of creating the board is what's important.

Choosing how to lay out your board is also up to your discretion. You could treat your board like a chronological road map showing how you want your journey to unfold. Possibly making a creative collage speaks to you more. I've created my boards both ways and have not found one way to be superior. Again, focus on the energy, intention, and uniqueness of your board over minute details.

When creating your intentional power board, not only would you incorporate specific images like a pregnant woman to represent yourself, but metaphorical images play an integral part in the board process. As shared by neuroscientist Tara Swart in her book "The Source," metaphorical images trigger the emotional subconscious part of your brain along with the logical conscious side. Relating to conception, you could choose pictures of seeds or perhaps incorporate a packet of seeds of your favorite flower and place it on your board. The seeds signify you're planting the seed, the idea of conception. Another idea can be an image of a flower blooming to represent a baby blooming and growing in your womb.

When creating your board, take all the time you need. Be present, intentional, and authentic about the items you place on your board.

Think about what each image means to you and write a note to include it with the image, or write about each image in your journal.

It's important to note that everyone's journey to motherhood is different. Whatever avenue that may be, including IVF or adoption, it's your story to foster and tell. These same principles apply. Put on your board what you want your family's result to be. Design your baby's nursery and put a pretend baby in your arms. If you're adopting, place an image of the completed adoption papers on your board.

Your board is not a set-it-and-forget-it approach. Tara Swart also suggests that "you create an action board to prime your brain to grasp any opportunities that will bring you closer to what you've identified as your goal in life." This board will remind you to act and do the proper things to attract what you want. For example, how are you preparing your body to conceive? Do you stay up until the wee hours of the morning partying with your friends? Or are you resting and nurturing your body to create a healthy and safe space for the soul to enter?

Ideally, look at your board multiple times a day even if your board is via an online source. Recall the importance and power of mental rehearsal. Mentally rehearse these images and intentions coming true on your board. The board's purpose is to strengthen the neuropathways in your brain to create the reality you desire, as repetition does this, just as you learned in the mental rehearsal section of the 'Mindful Mama' chapter.

Journaling

As you've learned in this book, journaling has many profound impacts. It's also a fantastic way to connect with the spirit of your unborn child. The term 'Spirit Baby' refers to the spirit of a child ready to be born, who has already chosen its parents, and whose spirit lingers in one of the parents' auras. At this stage, the parents need to engage in the physical aspect of bringing the child from the spirit to the physical realm. If a baby's spirit is waiting to connect with its parents, I believe journaling can help lead the spirit to its parents, who are ready to welcome them. This is a powerful practice for those who are undergoing IVF or choosing adoption to add to or complete their family.

I wrote to my son before conception and talked to him as if he were right in front of me. I also journaled throughout my pregnancy and shared with him milestones, doctor visits, and anything else we thought was important to share or document. Sometimes, I just wrote to him to tell him how excited we were to meet him. These journals will be a great memento to give to him one day when he is older. I hope he enjoys reading through them as much as I enjoyed writing to him.

Desiring something deeply, such as becoming pregnant, can greatly test our patience and optimism. This is especially true if you've faced the heartbreak of a miscarriage, find the process taking longer than anticipated, or fear that your biological clock is running out. Release your worries and past struggles and concentrate on the present and the aspects within your control. While you can influence how you prepare for conception, the timing of when it occurs is out of your hands. Embrace the insights provided in this chapter as your guiding light and have faith that what is meant for you will come in its own time; remember, timing is everything.

CHAPTER 9

The Butterfly Effect

The Butterfly Effect is defined as a small action that has a profound impact on your life overall.

Motherhood is a transformational journey, much like the caterpillar's evolution into a butterfly. As the caterpillar hatches from its egg, its primary focus is on nourishment, even consuming the eggshell from which it emerged. This feeding stage, a period of intense growth, sees the caterpillar shed its old skin multiple times, making way for its new, larger self. It can increase its size by 100 times in weeks, growing up to two inches.

The caterpillar then embarks on its chrysalis period, a time of rapid metamorphosis and self-renewal. The caterpillar has completely transformed in just a few days, emerging as a beautiful butterfly. The butterfly then unfurls its wings, breaks free from its cocoon, and takes flight, revealing its unique and vibrant colors, contributing to the masterpiece of nature.

Every aspect of a caterpillar's journey to becoming a butterfly mirrors your transition to motherhood. When the caterpillar emerges from its egg, its main goal is nourishment. This chapter is devoted to that process.

Incubation Period

On airplanes, you are reminded to prioritize your own well-being. During the safety briefing, it is announced, "...Make sure to secure your own mask before helping others." Why is this message significant? If you become unconscious, you cannot assist anyone else. So why do we live our lives in an unconscious state? Similarly, the saying, "You can't pour from an empty cup," yet we continue this behavior? Many of us fall into this trap, some more than others. It's crucial to recognize when you're helping others at your own expense. It's your job to make sure your cup is full. If you don't know your love language, now is the time to discover it, and if someone else isn't helping fill your cup, make sure you're filling it yourself and even allowing it to overflow abundantly. You are rewiring the narrative of motherhood that suggests we must neglect ourselves in favor of our family. This idea is inherently contradictory, so let's work together to challenge this perspective. You deserve much more than this.

Embracing motherhood begins with learning to mother yourself first. The core of mothering involves being nurturing, protective, and compassionate. You must learn to prioritize your needs. If you're uncertain about how to care for yourself, start by allowing yourself to rest when necessary. Remember, rest is a form of productivity. Society influences us to think that constant busyness and multitasking equate to success, but in reality, the opposite is often true. If you find yourself continuously active, consider this a cue to slow down and prioritize your well-being. One of the most effective ways to look after yourself is to maintain balance as much as possible, as you've previously learned.

Caring for yourself involves balancing rest with movement. Staying active will strengthen your body for pregnancy and childbirth. (Always ensure that your healthcare provider has approved your ability to exercise.) Walking is a fantastic way to physically nurture yourself and comes with numerous health advantages, particularly during pregnancy. While I was expecting, I dedicated myself to walking 10-15 miles each week outdoors, and I experienced numerous benefits, many of which I believe stemmed from my time in nature. I did walking meditations and listened to insightful books and podcasts that educated me on pregnancy and birth. I utilized this time for relaxation and learning.

I also committed to a consistent prenatal yoga routine, incorporating visualizations and breathwork, training my mind and body for childbirth. Additionally, purposeful strength training and lower-impact HIIT (high-intensity interval training) workouts provided me with the endurance, mobility, and vigor necessary to carry me through the last few weeks of pregnancy and for birth. When I was giving birth, the preparation and practice I had done allowed me to slip my mind and body into its routine, giving me the confidence I needed. For access to my favorite workouts that supported my pregnancy, visit www.melbraun.com.

In addition to physically caring for your body, you must do the same for your mind. You now recognize that external energies can influence your internal experience but remember your internal state creates your outside world. Establish mindfulness routines, refer to the 'Mindful Mama' chapter, and be attentive to what you allow into your mental space. If you find yourself feeling restless at bedtime after watching the news, consider stopping this habit in the evening and choosing a different time during the day to catch up. Instead, finish your day with a personal development book or something that brings you joy or motivation. Choose to implement meditation before bed, which can help you relax after the day's events, or give yourself Reiki to unwind.

I personally avoid watching the news. Instead, I subscribe to a news outlet that sends updates via email. Each morning, I evaluate whether I'm in the right headspace to read the topics highlighted for the day. Often, I don't even open the email and simply delete it from my inbox. As an empath, I find that watching the news and consuming too much social media significantly affects me. Therefore, I'm very selective about the accounts I follow, considering how they will impact my mental state and energy levels.

As for your energy, you learned in the 'Your Energy Body' chapter that safeguarding and preserving yourself energetically will, in turn, protect you physically. Lean on the tools provided in the chapter, 'Energetic Responsibility,' and implement the methods given or additional ones you find suitable for yourself. Focusing on shielding your energy body will help optimize your overall well-being.

A key aspect of motherhood is showing kindness and compassion, especially towards yourself. Have you noticed how a mother's enthusiasm and encouragement soar when her child is striving for milestones like crawling or walking? The praise and acknowledgment given for these achievements are remarkable. I urge you to be a cheerleader for yourself, celebrating milestones, whether big or small, because they all matter, just as you will for your child. Additionally, choose your words wisely when speaking to your child and yourself. Remember that your words possess a unique frequency, and both your mind and body become attuned to how you communicate with yourself. This is especially true during pregnancy. Create a list of intentional and positive affirmations you can recite throughout the day. If you struggle to come up with your own list of affirmations, visit www.melbraun.com to download a free copy of my favorite affirmations and the ones I used throughout my pregnancy and birth.

This incubation period is non-negotiable. Establishing nourishing habits before your baby arrives significantly increases the likelihood of sustaining a healthy routine afterward.

Find Your Tribe

As you prepare for motherhood and giving birth, take time to consider who your tribe is. Whose support and energy will serve you best as you become a mother? Who will advocate for what you need? Who will be your cheerleader when you feel overwhelmed, discouraged, or defeated? Who will offer you a comfortable shoulder to cry on or be your sounding board if needed? You want these rock stars to lift you up and keep you on track—your good vibe tribe.

Nothing happens by chance. A doula settled into what I referred to as the "healing hallway," where I saw Reiki clients. Over several months, we became acquainted, and, rather ironically, I found out I was pregnant around six months after we first met. After informing our families, she was among the first to learn our news. Her client list was filled well beforehand, and I just managed to secure one of her last client spots for my due date.

I intended to deliver at a nearby hospital since my regular provider was affiliated with that facility. Following my initial pregnancy confirmation visit, I returned for my eight-week check-up, where my age labeled me as a "Mature Mother." My provider, whom I adored, told me that not only would I have regular check-ups with her, but I would also need to see a specialist during my pregnancy. This news took me back since I had no health issues and wasn't on any medication, yet I was being categorized as high-risk simply due to my age. It seemed unfair to be treated as if I were in a risky situation when I was a healthy, mature woman excited to become a mother.

Feeling discouraged by the treatment that lay ahead for my pregnancy, I reached out to my doula to tell her what had happened. This is when I was introduced to the idea of going to the birthing center. I envisioned an unmedicated birth, no matter the setting. My husband and I scheduled a tour of the facility and instantly fell in love with the environment, the staff, and the care we'd receive. I felt this place viewed me as a unique mother-to-be, not another number.

Following the tour, I transitioned my care from my usual provider to the birthing center and began attending regular appointments there. During each visit, we got to know the staff by name, built relationships with them, and met various midwives to familiarize ourselves with each one, since we would not know who would be on duty the day my son would arrive. It was my ideal situation and truly felt like home.

My doula consistently emphasized that I had the power to make choices that were best for me and my baby. When it was suggested multiple times that I take daily aspirin due to my age and increased risk for preeclampsia, I graciously declined. I had never experienced high blood pressure and informed them that I would consider it only if my blood pressure became an issue. Throughout my pregnancy, my blood pressure remained excellent, and I never needed to take aspirin.

During my pregnancy, I stayed in touch with my doula, who clarified topics we needed to consider. Our family aimed to make informed decisions while staying holistic, and she guided us effectively in that balance. She respected our viewpoints, refrained from imposing her personal beliefs, and instead offered credible resources for our choices. Her support instilled confidence that we were deciding what was best for us and our son.

She consistently supported my birth plan, acting as my cheerleader and confidant in the weeks before the birth. My birthing experience was magical and aligned perfectly with my vision. Her collaboration played a significant role in the success of my birth story, and I am eternally grateful I had her as a part of my tribe.

It's important to find your tribe that will advocate for you, and empower you, ensuring your pregnancy and birthing story unfolds as you desire. If your doctor and/ or the facility doesn't align with you and your family, switch. Seek alternatives if you feel unsupported or unheard. If you believe a doula will enhance your birthing experience, hire one. For us, it was one of the best investments and paid dividends even during my postpartum period. This is your story; don't let others dictate otherwise.

There's also something special about connecting with other expectant mothers. Understanding what each other is going through in real-time. If you don't have anyone you know that is expecting, I encourage you to find others via online groups or look into classes and group gatherings being offered where you're choosing to give birth.

Boundaries

Safeguarding my energy is non-negotiable for me, especially during my pregnancy. This led me to adopt the "keep your eyes on your own paper" approach. This strategy proved extremely beneficial and significantly contributed to my positive pregnancy and birth experience.

For whatever reason, once I found out I was pregnant, women came out of the woodwork, sharing their unfortunate birth experiences with me. Because I was hyper-focused on preserving my energy and positive mindset, there were times I would either remove myself from the conversation (this is easier than you think when there's always a baby pressing on your bladder) or I would respond to those eager to share with, "I'm really sorry your experience didn't meet your expectations and appreciate that I am a safe space for you wanting to share, but my pregnancy is centered around energetics and mindfulness, so I kindly ask for you to refrain from giving details that were upsetting for you." Their response to this was always well respected and received once they understood my reasoning for not wanting to bring their experiences into my sphere of influence.

Although I spent a lot of time educating myself about pregnancy and the birth process, I was also very mindful of what I listened to. Certain birthing podcasts had been recommended to me, and I was shocked by the number of devastating stories shared; again, they did not align with the energy I was creating within and around me. I started to pre-screen if a podcast was suitable for me, whether it was asking the person who sent it to me what it was about or scanning through the podcast first before listening to it.

In addition to establishing boundaries around hearing unsatisfactory birth experiences, once learning I was pregnant, the social media algorithms inundated my feed with pregnancy posts; positive ones, disturbing ones, and my favorite, supermodel-looking moms, who still had abs at six months pregnant. I must say, rock on to those mamas out there, but what was being portrayed was not what pregnancy looked like for me.

In the times I was feeling inferior to others, potentially photoshopped or not, I reminded myself this was not anyone else's body, pregnancy, or journey. This was my unique experience, and I consciously treated it as such. I became very mindful of what posts I would spend time reading or scrolling through, and I also cut back on my time on social media and even unfollowed some accounts that were not serving me energetically. I was growing life within me not only physically healthy but also an energetically aligned life. I viewed my baby and me as an inseparable team.

I faced external pressures as well. People continually projected their concerns and fears onto me, running through various "what if" scenarios. This concern largely stemmed from my decision to give birth at a birthing center instead of a traditional hospital. Questions like, "What if something goes wrong? How close are you to a real hospital?" and "What if there's a medical emergency?" surfaced often. Many would remind me that the birthing center was an hour away and ponder what would happen if I didn't arrive on time. I recognize their intentions came from genuine concern; they only wanted what was best for me, and their worries were legitimate from their perspective. However, I needed to consider how these concerns impacted me personally.

I wasn't oblivious to factors other than my mental rehearsal plan; I chose not to fixate on them. Instead, I remained proactive with my thoughts. I continued to see the possibilities of everything that could and would go right instead of the potential limitations that would derail my ideal birth. I had assembled a trusted tribe of people to deliver the best possible outcome for my birth plan that supported me and my baby. I educated myself and those concerned about the birthing center's protocols and clarified how my pregnancy was energetic and mindset driven. For any remaining questions, I directed them to my husband, who was great at addressing their concerns.

I remained careful about who I spent my time with. If I noticed someone being consistently negative or gossipy, I politely declined their invitation to get together. It's perfectly fine to say no, especially when prioritizing your well-being and that of your baby. As you will learn in the 'Baby Communication' chapter, your emotions influence your baby's feelings. Safeguard your energy, surround yourself with positivity, and establish clear boundaries. I promise you won't regret it.

Surrender: Learn to trust the Universe like a baby trusts its caretaker.

Have you ever really watched how a baby instinctively relies on their caregiver? Knowing when they cry because they are hungry, they will be fed. Believing that you will nurture them at just the right time when they need it the most. They trust that when you pick them up and carry them around, you will secure them tightly and not let them fall. This is the same level of faith we need to place in the Universe.

Surrendering naturally poses a significant challenge for many because the desire to control outcomes often stems from fear. It's important to let go of the need for control and learn to embrace life's ebb and flow. There are moments in life and throughout motherhood when things change unexpectedly despite having a well-laid plan, rendering all your careful calculations irrelevant. When situations don't unfold as anticipated, remember that you've surrendered and done your utmost to manage what you could. Stay optimistic that everything is aligning perfectly in divine timing for your greater good and continue to concentrate on your mental rehearsals and intentional positive affirmations. Typically, outcomes turn out even better than you had envisioned. While it might take a while to recognize the silver lining, realize that what seems to happen to you is often happening for you, and the Universe had your back all along. These experiences can either upset you or empower you. It requires considerable courage to let go and flow.

It's great to know you want and need to surrender, but how do you learn to surrender if you've always been a control freak? The answer is mindfulness. Whenever you feel yourself trying to control the outcome of things, revert to the practices in the 'Mindful Mama' chapter.

The Final Few Weeks

Everyone you ask will confirm just how tough the final few weeks of pregnancy can be. The physical changes your body undergoes inevitably impact your mental state. You may find yourself more swollen, sleep becomes increasingly difficult, and if your baby is positioned low, you may experience sharper back pain, and these symptoms multiply as your body gears up for childbirth. Personally, three weeks prior to my due date, I noticed signs that labor could begin at any moment with bloody show, heavier mucus, and prodromal labor, yet my son remained cozy inside my womb. I reminded myself that my journey and pregnancy were uniquely mine, and that my son would arrive when he was ready, but that reassurance didn't alleviate my mental struggle. During this time, my husband was home for an extended mid-season break, which coincided with the final weeks of my pregnancy. We felt up against the clock of his upcoming departure to return to work, igniting fears that he might miss our son's birth.

The final few weeks of my pregnancy challenged me in new ways mentally, emotionally, and spiritually. The mental scrimmage of excitement to hurry things along because I was so ready to meet my son, yet I had to balance patience and continue to wait. I was already posing traits of motherly instincts to put my son's needs before my own, deep down genuinely wanting what was best for him over what I wanted. The idea was that I needed to do something else to continue to "prepare" although everything was set. I had to shift my focus to just be. Be and embrace the stillness. Sitting with this stillness showed me how far I'd come in embracing the quiet and being comfortable with myself and my thoughts. Instead of playing out the "what ifs" that could happen within the next few hours, days, or weeks, I was able to take my focus to visualize "how" I wanted things to happen and direct my energy towards the outcomes I wanted.

Emotionally, I realized I was getting ready to shed a part of me that had served me for 36 years of my life. The growth I was undergoing was inevitable, like the feeding stage of a caterpillar shedding its old skin multiple times to make way for its new, larger self. However, the slight fear of discomfort I would experience inside as I grew into this new way of life triggered the old internal dialogue of "Would I be good enough?" I quickly realized what was happening, and I was not afraid of the unknown like I once was. I now flowed with the ways of life like the tides of the ocean, and this would be no different.

I then found myself in the chrysalis period, hibernating until my son's arrival, yet realizing the rapid metamorphosis that would happen within a few days, as my son would be ready to leave the cocoon of my womb, and take flight into the world with me, as we embarked on this journey of mother and son for the first time together.

Spiritually, I felt more connected than ever. I had been shown throughout this entire process how I was continually supported, even on the days I felt alone. I had been guided every step of the way and was reminded by Source and my higher self, that this moment in time would be no different. In meditation, I would continue to hear, "Trust the process, trust your body, trust the timing." Trust used to be difficult for me, but I knew now more than ever what would empower me the most, was to fully surrender. To let go of all expectations and potential outcomes and to remain present in each moment as there were deeper meanings and teachings in the present than focusing on the future.

It was in these final weeks that I realized I had begun preparing for this moment a decade before it actually happened. I was eternally grateful for the emotional healing I had done up to this point, the exploration of holistic modalities, the mindfulness practices I now had as a routine, and my commitment to physical fitness. It was at this moment I realized my confidence to fully embark on the journey of motherhood, backed by my supportive team to help me. The butterfly effect had come to completion, and I was ready to fly.

CHAPTER 10

Good Vibe Tribe

This chapter is entirely focused on the mama's supporters. Your contribution is an essential piece of the overall support system for the mother. You might feel unsure about your role and how to fulfill it, which can be overwhelming. However, this chapter aims to equip you for success and boost your confidence to become the best supporter possible.

You are the backbone of support for her, whether you are her partner, parent, friend, co-worker, or someone from a support group. She needs reassurance that she can reach out to you any time—day or night—and trust you to be there through all situations. This could mean satisfying her late-night cravings with a milkshake from her favorite ice cream shop, preparing a soothing warm Epsom salt bath to alleviate her discomfort, or ensuring she doesn't miss your regular nature walk together to uplift her spirits.

You serve as her mindset trainer during moments of doubt. As her accountability partner, you help her maintain her self-care routine and yoga practice. You're also her emotional and energetic coach, ready to answer her calls and offer an empathetic ear. You confirm she is respecting her energy body as she thoughtfully considers how and with whom she spends her time. Ensure she feels safe and nurtured because those emotions carry over to her baby as you will learn in the next chapter.

Being a confidant carries significant responsibility, particularly in communication with the mother. This is true during her pregnancy and even more so in the postpartum period. You've already discovered how hormonal fluctuations can affect behavior and reactions, so it's important to avoid adding unnecessary stress for all parties through your choice of words or delivery. Remember, words carry a unique frequency, so when communicating with the mother, choose your words wisely. Here is a story a mother shared with me about her experience with her support system.

I had a Reiki client who was eagerly expecting her first child. In her circle of friends, many had recently become parents, so she sought their advice, having just experienced childbirth. Her goal was to have an unmedicated delivery in a hospital setting. After confirming her pregnancy, I referred her to my doula, whom she eventually hired to help facilitate her birth plan.

During one of her Reiki sessions, she shared that when she expressed her intention of having an unmedicated birth, her friends mocked her and asked what she felt she needed to prove. My client was taken back by their reactions, as they insisted that epidurals existed for a reason and couldn't comprehend why she was pursuing what they considered the 'more challenging way to give birth.' Since I had recently gone through pregnancy and birth and was in the middle of writing this book, I inadvertently became her "coach," so to speak. I told her the "keep your eyes on your paper approach" and reminded her that this was her body, her baby, her journey and that she should not allow outside influences to dictate otherwise. I stressed the significance of "Her Tribe" and encouraged her to communicate with them her commitment to her pregnancy and birth being a mindful and energetic experience. Post conversation she could choose to keep them at a distance if they failed to respond with the necessary respect. This didn't need to be permanent, just during this important period.

Reiki helped her feel calmer, rather than reactive to the situation, which gave her a clear headspace to express to her friends how their comments affected her negatively. Of course, it was never their intention to hurt her feelings; they thought they were being helpful by encouraging her to receive an epidural instead. This open dialogue eased tensions and reinforced her sense of support from her friends. Five months later, she experienced the unmedicated birth she wanted and welcomed a beautiful, healthy baby girl.

This illustrates how her friends believed they were contributing positively, yet they detracted from the situation. When discussing with my Reiki client post conversation with her friends, she mentioned it would have been more beneficial if they had asked questions about her desire for an unmedicated birth and shown more curiosity about the process and what she was doing to prepare for it.

Personally, I've learned over the years that my suggestions or comments, intended to be helpful like my Reiki client's friends, often escalated tensions. Learning from my lessons, I now focus on listening to others and considering their viewpoints. Rather than imposing my opinion or comment, I ask if they would like to hear my view of the situation, or I share what has worked for me. Then, I allow them to determine if my experience might suit their needs, avoiding any sense of pressure to follow my path.

If you're supporting a mother through a situation that may not align with your preferences or understanding, take some time to learn about her choices for childbirth, parenting style, or any new information she is providing. This effort will demonstrate your engagement, support, and genuine desire to offer the care she needs. Take time to research unfamiliar topics and visit the birthing facility's website to understand their processes and procedures. As a first-time mom, she faces a whirlwind of decisions for her baby, so affirming her choices, as they feel right to her, will give her the boost of confidence she needs as she navigates this unfamiliar terrain.

As the supporter, your main focus should be to limit her stress and anxiety as much as possible. This is particularly relevant towards the end of her pregnancy, as discomfort significantly increases. She is likely ready for her baby to arrive so she can experience some relief, but she may also feel anxious about becoming a mother. It's advisable to limit frequent inquiries about the baby's arrival as it might only heighten her anxiety and fear. If you know she is struggling with anxiety related to the end of pregnancy, childbirth, or the postpartum period, consider gifting them a journal. Personalize it with an encouraging message, like, "You've got this, Mama," or their name. This journal can help them soothe their racing thoughts, providing comfort for both them and their baby. Gifting them a journal can genuinely assist in easing their fears and empower them during this journey. Maybe they would like journaling to their baby as a way of deepening their connection with them.

Keeping the mama balanced and relaxed throughout her pregnancy and postpartum is a priority. Allow the mother some time to choose what she wishes to do. She might want to enjoy a pedicure, take a nap, read a book or magazine, go for a walk, or attend a prenatal class. If local classes aren't available or easily accessible, visit www.melbraun.com for prenatal support.

It's a delicate dance of knowing when to offer suggestions, ask questions, or help, but bettering your skills as an observer will help guide you on when to step in and when to not.

Take a moment to think about the point you're trying to get across or the question you want to ask, and thoroughly think through them before presenting them to the mother. Once you know the question you want to ask or the statement you want to share, put yourself in the mother's shoes and think about how your question or comment would make her feel. I will also add that timing can affect how the mother may respond, so if you can tell she seems a little more sensitive that day, refrain from asking her a question at that moment. Another suggestion is not to ask the mother at all and to ask the person who is their main supporter, like their partner, the question.

Medical Professional

If you're reading this book and you're a medical professional, whether that be a nurse, doctor, or midwife, I want to express the importance of giving respectful care to the mother and her baby. This may be your 1,000th birth experience, but it may be this mother's first. She and her baby are not just another number; they are miracles working together to bring life into this world, and they should be treated as such. Especially if the plan deviates from her original birthing plan, it is your duty to make sure she continues to feel heard and safe. You are an integral part of her birthing memories, so please leave a positive mark on it.

Partner of the Mom

I want to highlight the mother's partner. Your contributions do not go unnoticed, even if they aren't always acknowledged. My husband excelled at juggling his work and travel while nurturing me whenever possible. He didn't just give foot rubs; he was actively involved, constantly asking how he could help, inquiring about our son's size on the tracking app, and when home during my third trimester, he catered to my endless nesting desires—like my urge to clean the house thoroughly before our son's arrival. With his delightful humor, he joked, "Do you really think our son will come home and say, 'Oh my goodness, Mom! The baseboards have a speck of dust!'?" Nesting can take over your mind, but he happily tackled my "Preparing for his arrival honey-do list" with a smile.

As the mother's partner, I want to recognize the mental and emotional stress you experience while supporting them in the lead-up to labor, during labor, and throughout your birth.

In the final weeks before our son's birth, my husband and I experienced a real emotional seesaw. One day, I was fully surrendered, while he was anxious about potentially missing the birth as his departure date drew near; the next day, I was a crying hot mess while he remained calm and composed. This emotional rollercoaster took a toll on both of our nervous systems.

The morning my water broke was quite an adventure. I had only managed to catch a couple of hours of sleep, while my husband got about five. I recall our doula asking him how he felt seeing me in pain, knowing he couldn't do much to help; he seemed uncertain at first and then replied, "I've never really seen her in pain. Mel's so tough!" Through my laboring in the car on the way to the birthing center and while laboring there, he was so calm and supportive, as he held my hand during each contraction. He appeared to handle watching me in pain well.

While in the birthing pool, I also recalled my doula asking him if he was okay with blood, and he admitted he had a small worry about possibly passing out. However, when it came time for our son to make his grand entrance, he looked down at the mirror alongside me, which was placed in the water, as we watched in awe at the amazing moment of our son being born. It was incredible to see him, who once mentioned a fear of blood, confidently grab the umbilical cord and cut it after all the blood had thoroughly pumped through.

After departing that afternoon for his event, he enjoyed eleven hours of uninterrupted sleep, whereas I had only a few. I believe it's essential to highlight this because, while your partner may not have physically done the work you did, the mental, emotional, and spiritual support they provide is taxing.

Regardless of the situation, my husband was always there for me, and he continues to be every day. He jumped into the chaos of parenthood with me full force. This support is not only vital for me but also crucial for our son. During my pregnancy, feeling safe and nurtured meant that our son experienced this in the womb, as discussed in the 'Baby Communication' chapter. Now that he is nearly fourteen months old while I write this, my husband's ongoing presence enables our son to feel secure in discovering who he is meant to be, which is an incredible gift.

As the partner of the mom, you're an integral piece to the puzzle. It takes a team and a village at times, and we, as the mothers, appreciate you intentionally showing up for us. Thank you for all that you do.

Mom to Mom

If you're a supporter of the new mother, who is also a mother, constantly sharing about how you did things a certain way isn't usually helpful. Even though your intentions are pure, allow her to become a mother at her own pace, in her own way, just as you did. Remember, every mother and baby is unique, and what worked for you may not work for her. Things change quickly, especially in the baby world, with the resources now available and the advances in technology, we continue to gain a deeper understanding of their developing needs.

What you can do to help is educate yourself on how she is choosing to mother and support her this way. For example, 30 years ago, there was no information on babies' sleep. Mothers put their babies to bed when they thought it was best, usually when they were going to bed themselves. Today, many mothers focus on wake windows to make sure their babies are well-rested and avoid them being overly tired, which studies now show disrupts their sleep. Instead of telling the new mom how you used to do things, ask her what she's reading about the wake windows so you can learn how to support her best and her baby and their habits.

When I was born in the late 1980s, many mothers utilized the "cry it out method" to help their babies sleep. After completing the bedtime routine, they would place the baby in the crib, letting them cry until they eventually wore themselves out and fell asleep. While I don't judge this method if it works for your family, many mothers today, me included, lean towards a gentler approach. I decided to bedshare with my son until he was 4.5 months old, which allowed me to rest better while breastfeeding as he snuggled beside me. Our choice to bedshare was also shaped by epigenetics, referenced in the 'Emotional Body' chapter. Having carried my son for nearly ten months, I recognized he was experiencing an adjustment period to life now outside my womb. I knew we would eventually transition him to his crib, and by nurturing his needs from the beginning, I believed that the process would go smoothly. He learned he could count on me by building trust that I would always be there for him.

When we moved him from our bed to his crib, he cried, but it wasn't at the level our sleep coach had cautioned; she was surprised at how easily he adjusted. I believe this was due to the Reiki I provided, which helped soothe his nervous system and the assurance he received from me in the months leading up to the transition.

Even now, at fourteen months old, when he cries during the night for various reasons, I pick him up and soothe him. I can tell he has calmed down when he takes two deep exhales, indicating he has reset. When I place him back in his crib, he may cry for about 20 seconds but then drifts back to sleep.

Rather than criticizing families who opt for bed sharing, it's important to understand their reasons and offer guidance on safe practices. From my experience, I've observed that many countries prefer to keep their babies close during infancy and even into the toddler stage. Ultimately, it's about selecting what works best for you and your family. As the supporter, being respectful of how the new mom is choosing to mother, will deepen your connection to her rather than drive a wedge.

Baby Shower and Post Birth

Baby showers are an exciting time for the mother and those closest to her to celebrate her baby. As she spends time preparing her gift registry list, she inevitably forgets to include a few things that would make her comfortable during her transition into postpartum. When attending a baby shower, I always make sure to have a special little something for the mom. I've gifted a luscious belly butter to help with the itching that is induced by their growing belly, cozy pajamas that make breastfeeding more accessible, or treat them to a prenatal massage. Gifting chiropractic care is another great idea, especially to one who holds a certification in the Webster Technique.

This will help with the expectant mother's ailments and help keep her pelvis aligned, assisting with an easier birth. Chiropractic care can also help with fetal positioning if the baby needs help getting into a better position for delivery.

The same goes for the mother post-birth. When calling to check in or coming to visit, ask about the mom. How is she doing and ask her what she needs. Everyone is always hyper-focused on the baby, which can leave the mother feeling left in the dark, and as the supporter, you're there to cater to her.

And one more bonus for the mother is on the day her baby turns one, do something a little extra special for her or give her a commemorative gift. This day not only marks her baby's milestone but is also the day she birthed a new version of herself, and that, too, deserves celebration.

Magic Mama Meals

One of the greatest gifts you can give a mother is to help feed her as she becomes a mother. Keeping her nourished, especially during the first few months, is essential to her recovery and her baby's development.

During my pregnancy with my son, a close friend who had three kids recognized how vital support was during the postpartum period. She dedicated time to preparing meals for my husband and me to make this transitional time easier. When she visited to photograph our newborn son, she brought a cooler filled with ready-to-eat meals, which we stored in our freezer for days when cooking felt too exhausting. These meals proved invaluable on several occasions, inspiring me to prepare meals for every expecting mother I knew going forward to offer them nourishment.

In Chinese medicine, a pregnant woman experiences a yang, warm energy state due to increased blood flow supporting her and her developing baby. During childbirth, blood loss is a loss of chi (life force energy) that contributes warmth and protection. This blood loss transitions her body's chi from yang to yin, cool energy, leading to a depletion of yang energy. Maintaining a balance of yin and yang energy is crucial. Since women are more yin energy by nature, providing the new mother with nutritious yang (warm) foods can help replenish her yang energy, assisting in restoring her chi to a balanced state, which promotes physical recovery.

You can begin taking her nourishing meals as early as when she's in the hospital. Better yet, it should be readily available as her first meal after delivery when recovering. She is depleted from giving birth and needs to be replenished with healthy nutrients. These will also serve as the baby's first nutrients through her colostrum and milk. If having these meals accessible at the hospital isn't an option, ensure they are available once she returns home.

I not only prepare the meals, but I also include inspirational messages on the packaging and provide 'date night' questions for parents to foster connection and conversation. Especially in the early months with a newborn, it can be easy to lose sight of maintaining a healthy relationship with your partner, allowing every moment to revolve around the baby. However, sustaining a healthy connection with your partner is crucial for mental, emotional, and physical recovery; as discussed earlier in this book, everything is intrinsically linked.

When preparing meals for a new mother, prioritize foods that promote healing. Dishes that provide warmth, such as stews and soups made with bone broth, are particularly beneficial during postpartum recovery. Bone broth contains gelatin, which aids in repairing connective tissue and reducing excessive bleeding after childbirth. Additionally, focus on meals rich in quality proteins that are packed with iron, calcium, and magnesium. Remember, food serves as medicine.

If a mother is breastfeeding, it's best to avoid meals that contain gaseous foods like beans and cruciferous vegetables such as cabbage, broccoli, cauliflower, and kale. These items can lead to excess gas in the baby via the mother's milk, causing unnecessary discomfort for the infant.

For a list of nutritionally rich foods that aid in the mother's recovery, visit www.melbraun.com and search under the "Magic Mama" tab. I'd love to see how you're nourishing and caring for the new mother, tag me at @magicmamabook and use hashtag #magicmamameals.

House Support – don't assume they have help

When you're dropping off your magic mama meals, use this time as an opportunity to check in with the mother. Instead of asking how they are feeling, which is likely sore, especially if they've had a cesarean section, tired, and overwhelmed, ask them what you can do to help. Don't be surprised if they have no idea on what you can do to help. I remember in my early postpartum period, I was running off only a few hours of sleep most days and couldn't remember if I had brushed my teeth, let alone my hair.

If you notice dishes in the sink, just wash them. If they have a dog, consider asking if you can take it for a walk. Depending on her recovery progress, you might also ask if she'd like to join you for some fresh air. Perhaps she would appreciate you watching her baby for 15-20 minutes, allowing her to walk alone or enjoy an uninterrupted shower. I do want to mention that it's important not to take it personally if she doesn't want to leave her baby with you or even let you hold her baby. I wanted my son to be with me as much as possible, and when he wasn't, I felt like a part of me was missing when he wasn't by my side. I never anticipated my postpartum experience to unfold this way; I thought I would cherish my alone time like always. Instead, I would let someone hold him just long enough to shower and, on some days, get some extra sleep. Remember, as the supporter, you want to do things that induce relaxation and rehabilitation, not create stress, and don't be surprised if what she wanted one day changes the next. That is all part of the re-balancing period of her hormones.

There were days during my postpartum period I didn't feel like talking to anyone and communicating my needs fell under that category. Something I wish I would've done that I am now providing you, is a list of tasks for visitors to do when they were there. Luckily for you, I've already compiled a list for you to use and add to for personal use. You can download this checklist at www.melbraun.com.

As the mother's supporter, remember that your contributions are appreciated, even if thanks aren't always expressed. You're doing amazing by being present and providing support and comfort whenever possible. From my own experience during pregnancy and the postpartum phase, I can assure you that your efforts truly make a difference.

CHAPTER 11

Baby Communication

Fetal Origin

At this stage of the book, you've come to a deep understanding of how your energy, emotions, and mindset affect your physical body. Have you ever considered how these affect your child while in utero?

Your energy body continually emits electromagnetic waves. These waves serve as a means of communication not only with the world around you but also with your baby. This is why it is of the utmost importance to safeguard your energy as well as cleanse it, along with your environment, regularly. Ensuring you're healing your emotional body is integral to your mindset, which you are pre-programming into your baby.

Babies recall their mother's voice and the emotions she experienced while they were in utero. At about six months gestation, your baby's brain has developed enough to translate the messages you're sending them emotionally. You and your baby are constantly sharing an emotional dialogue. Every thought you have sends an emotional correspondence to your baby, programming their emotional behavior and response. While the occasional stressors won't dictate this, the continuation of stressful emotions or a profound loss can create an adverse side effect.

Much research has been performed on mothers who were in their second or third trimester and experienced a distressing event. This research aims to understand the effects of the event not only on the moms but also on their unborn babies. Scientists have used mice in some studies to evaluate such impacts.

Researchers from the University of Pennsylvania reported from their studies on mice that epigenetic markers can be altered due to environmental factors and can be transmitted through two generations of mice. This study on mice proposes that for mothers who had children in utero during a scarring event, the PTSD they experience from this occurrence will likely be passed onto their children and even grandchildren.

Some examples of this type of upsetting experience would include a mother being pregnant while surviving a natural disaster or terrorist attack, such as 9/11, the constant stress of financial difficulties or losing a family member. Depression or anxiety can originate in utero when the mother suffers a significant loss as it changes the chemical markers (epigenetics) in the baby's DNA. This is because the mother's focus becomes solely on processing their grief, distracting her from connecting with her unborn child. Or, the opposite can occur, where the mother numbs herself from experiencing the pain of grief, shutting off her conscious emotional connection with her baby. Charlotte, unfortunately, was one mother I know who experienced this.

I met Charlotte just a few months into my Reiki practice. Her initial session left such a strong impression that she decided to see me on a regular basis. During her sessions, we noticed a pattern of repressed anger and shame arising, emotions she was now consciously aware she felt during her distressful postpartum period. As she prioritized Reiki as her self-care regimen, she felt calmer and more at ease, allowing her to show up as her authentic self with her children. Due to these positive side effects, she eventually wanted to learn Reiki.

While attending my Reiki Master training, Charlotte experienced an incredible, energetic breakthrough. I was facilitating the session alongside my fellow students, and while focusing on her heart chakra, at the center of her chest, and her solar plexus right below, she began to release deep-seated emotions. Charlotte was letting go of the unbearable grief she had carried for the past five years. When she was six months pregnant with her oldest child, her grandmother, who was also her best friend, passed away. This agonizing loss led Charlotte to repress her grief, believing it was the right choice for herself and her unborn son. At that moment, she felt that embracing her grief would only cause more harm than good for them both. Plus, processing the grief would be a constant reminder that her grandmother was no longer physically with her, so she chose to contain her feelings instead.

For years, she endured inexplicable stomach discomfort, heart palpitations, and headaches stemming from the emotional scars of anger and shame from her postpartum period. Although these emotions had come up in our Reiki sessions, there was something about that day when she connected the dots. I believe it had to do with the attunement she received, when her higher consciousness knew she was ready and able to process and fully release these emotions.

As she sobbed on the table uncontrollably, we all held sacred, loving space for her as she released the grief from the loss of her grandmother, along with the anger and shame of the 'mom guilt' she felt during her vulnerable stages of postpartum. The guilt of not being the mother she aspired to be had solidified a narrative in her mind that she was a 'bad mom.' This perpetuated her intense anger patterns; being a child of the 1980s, she'd continually reminded herself she was 'bad' if she was angry. This subconscious cycle had been hard to break, but Reiki, in that moment, helped her unwire the stories she had told herself. That experience in the Reiki Master training was the revelation she needed to turn a corner.

Now a Reiki Master and practitioner within the community, she understands that the opposite is true. Fully grieving and releasing the emotions stored in her body would have greatly benefited both her and her children while they were in utero. Reiki, being the primary method she used, allowed Charlotte to find relief from her symptoms by bringing awareness to her energy body and identifying where those emotions were held. She came to realize that she was not only releasing the grief from the loss of her grandmother, but also the regret of not being the conscious mother she had wished to be. Reiki provided her with a sense of freedom from the guilt she'd carried for too long, along with her stomach discomfort, heart palpitations, and headaches.

Charlotte's children experience anxiety, ADHD, and sensitivity to stress. These symptoms reside in the heart chakra and solar plexus, exactly where Charlotte was carrying her repressed emotions. Luckily, Charlotte understands the energy body and incorporates Reiki as a fundamental practice in her home to give them the support they need. Since her commitment to using Reiki and mindfulness tools, she has noticed a tremendous difference in her children's health and behavior.

While Charlotte cannot change what her children experienced in utero, she can help clear them of these energies and give them the care they need today, allowing them the livelihood they deserve.

This is why Reiki is essential in helping you clear your PTSD or emotional imprints so your child's chemical markers are not altered from passing these experiences onto them. If you have emotional imprints that you wished you would've released before becoming pregnant or have already given birth, it's not too late. You can still cleanse these energies through Reiki for yourself and your child.

The Grid Clearing

I had my own experience of witnessing how emotions from my mother affected me in utero.

During my spiritual journey, years before becoming pregnant, the owners of 'The Nook,' where I attended intuitive development classes, suggested I book a 'Grid Clearing' session with them. This regression therapy, using hypnotherapy, would uncover the influences behind certain behaviors or patterns I exhibited. Not only did they guide me through the regression process, but they also cleared the energy associated with those behaviors or patterns. The intuitive gifts they had each cultivated over 50+ years of training were also a bonus to the session. Being keen on exploring various healing modalities, I was willing to try this and scheduled a session.

Upon arriving for the session, I settled into a chair facing them while they provided an overview of what to expect, emphasizing that every experience varied. As I gazed at the tissue box on the table before me, aware of how my body often responded to healing sessions with many tears, I reached for a few tissues and placed them in my lap.

The session began with them releasing specific energies around me, including an ex-boyfriend from before my husband. I was taken back when one of the owners mentioned my ex's name exactly. Although I was highly familiar with their intuitive abilities, her accuracy still surprised me. Since it had been more than a decade since we were together, I felt relieved to detach from that energy and cut those ties.

They then began the hypnotherapy part of the session by starting at my current age of 31. From there, I regressed to my early twenties and into my teenage years, where I had a lot of energy to clear. Next, I was taken back to my younger childhood, recalling a moment when my peers had left me alone in the woods on a cool fall day. The most impactful part of this regression therapy was seeing myself as a newborn and during my time in the womb.

I felt as if I were floating above, watching my mom cradle me in her arms, moments after my birth, while my dad stood nearby. I could tell both were relieved I was healthy, but neither seemed particularly joyful at that moment. My mother appeared to long for happiness, yet her anxiety over her lack of support overshadowed her feelings. At just 21, she struggled with her youth while facing adult responsibilities. My dad seemed burdened by the uncertainties of fatherhood, shaped by his own difficult childhood. As I floated above, I absorbed their emotions and reflected on their feelings; I wept in the present moment, mourning the emotions of apprehensiveness my parents exuded as I entered the world.

After gathering myself, the regression continued. I found myself in my mother's womb when she was seven months pregnant. I observed her petite stature and the growing size of her belly, noticing strangers approaching, eager to touch it. She managed a smile, pretending joy while caressing her belly during their conversations. Again, I sensed her relief that I was healthy, but her anxieties about the uncertain future took center stage. I watched intently, taking in the entire experience.

After the session, I collected my thoughts and called my mom to share what happened and ask some questions. As I recounted how the session started and walked her through the regression, I reached the part about my birth and time in utero. While describing what I felt and saw, my mom affirmed that what I had witnessed and experienced during my regression was indeed accurate.

While on the call, my mother shared her fears upon discovering she was pregnant. She worried about telling my father, especially since she already felt emotionally distant, and about revealing the news to her grandmother who had once suggested a hysterectomy as a wedding gift. (Incidentally, my mother ended up having a full hysterectomy at only 28.) She feared whether she would be accepted, along with the life growing inside her—me. The anxiety of the unknown loomed, compounded by her lack of support during pregnancy and after giving birth. This fear persisted into her postpartum period, particularly when her plan to stay home with me became financially unviable, forcing her to look for work outside the home.

At this point, my mother understood that she could rely solely on herself. Counting on others was not an option; no matter how challenging or demanding it became; she was determined to face it alone. This way, she would only have herself to hold accountable. My father had shown up the best he knew how at that time, but my mother needed more.

Once I empathized with my mother's vulnerable stories about her pregnancy and motherhood experience, everything clicked for me. When I received my very first energy session and was drowning in mucus and tears from the intense anger I felt, I realized at that moment I could never recall a memory that would've inflicted this anger because the anger I was feeling wasn't mine. It was my mother's that had been transferred to me. In that session, I was releasing her repressed anger that had been stored in my body.

I also realized that as a young, married adult, I possessed her same traits. Unconsciously aware, growing up in the environment of my strong, independent mother had programmed my psyche with these same qualities, which I had always admired. However, in my relationship with my husband, I recognized these qualities were to my detriment. I had firmly engrained in my mind I could only rely on myself despite my husband's repeated affirmations that we were a team.

This experience gave me a clear understanding of how a mother's emotions and environment influence her baby. I do not blame my parents for their emotional states during my development in the womb and beyond, particularly my mother. They both did the best they could given their own unhealed situations, and I am thankful for the effort they made for me throughout my childhood and continue to as an adult.

Once deciding I was ready to conceive, I recalled this experience and its impact on me. Now as a consciously aware woman, I promised myself I'd nurture my emotions, and when faced with lower vibrational emotions such as anger and fear, I would lean on Reiki to help discard them. I didn't let them fester within my body and, more importantly, affect my child in the womb and beyond.

Positive Communication

Positive influences can impact your baby in utero, just as negative ones do. Research indicates that mothers who maintain a positive outlook and look forward to their baby's arrival tend to have a child who stands a better chance of becoming emotionally stable. A mother's sense of safety and nurturing during pregnancy can create a reassuring environment for the baby, suggesting that this sense of security will continue once they are born. This highlights the significance of having your supportive tribe throughout your pregnancy journey. Similarly, feeling safe and nurtured during the postpartum phase and beyond will also positively affect your baby.

By eighteen weeks into pregnancy, a baby's hearing begins to develop. This allows you to connect with them not only emotionally and energetically but also verbally as they grow in the womb.

Theodor Geisel, more commonly known as 'Dr. Seuss' was extensively involved in prenatal research and found it fascinating. Researchers asked prospective parents to read the book, 'The Cat in the Hat,' aloud to their baby in utero. The research found that when this was done, there was an increase in uterine activity while the parents read to them, and the baby gradually settled down afterward. Once the baby was born, the parents reread the book, and the baby seemingly recalled the story since the baby had the same response out of the womb, just as they did in utero. This research indicates that learning and bonding with your child doesn't start once they are born; it begins in utero.

Not only did I frequently journal to my son while I was pregnant, but I deepened our bond by reading to him while he was in the womb. Knowing he was always listening, I had full conversations with him as if he was right before me, understanding every word. I would tell him about my day, what I was grateful for, talk about what size he was per my tracking app, say our positive affirmations aloud, 'We are healthy, we are strong, we are vibrant,' and what I was looking forward to once he was outside the womb. I would rub my belly when he'd kick, acknowledging his communication. Not only did this intrauterine bonding make me feel connected to him, but I've noticed it's deepened how I've been able to communicate with him telepathically once born.

Telepathic Communication

It had been a little over a week since we had transitioned our son from our bed to his crib, and he wasn't self-soothing as well as he had been. My logical brain thought he was crying because of the transition of him now sleeping alone. That was until I went back in there to rub his back and shush him when I heard him say, "You're not listening to me." In that instant, I had a clear knowing, claircognizance, he wasn't crying because he was alone; he was crying because he was in pain. He was teething. I picked him up from the crib, grabbed my teething oil, and rubbed it along his gums. I rocked him for a few minutes as he settled down, and his tears softened. I placed him back in the crib, rubbed his back a little more, and left the room. He fell asleep within minutes.

Two days after this incident of him telepathically communicating with me, his bottom teeth had broken through his gums.

Birth Story

Not only has my son telepathically communicated his needs with me after birth, but some of my favorite memories are when he communicated with me while in the womb, especially towards the end of my pregnancy.

The stress of waiting for my son's arrival was significant due to my husband's upcoming travel schedule. The window of him being home for the birth was narrowing down each day, and even though we hired a doula to be with me in case he wasn't home, we both would've regretted him missing such a monumental moment.

Nine days before my due date, it was getting harder to get restful sleep, so I napped as much as possible when I had the opportunity. After my morning walk, I felt quite tired and decided to lie down for a bit.

Upon waking, but still in that in-between stage of half awake, half asleep, I intuitively heard my son say, "Go with the flow. I'm coming." Once fully awake, I remembered the monarch butterfly that seemed to lead the way for a bit on our morning walk. Monarch butterflies are not only beautiful but symbolize transformation, renewal, and spiritual growth, all characteristics that were appropriate for the state I was in. I continued to remind myself that divine timing was truly everything, but that posed its challenges.

The next morning, my husband received a call that his schedule had changed. He was originally slated to be home until September 11th (my due date was the 13th), but now he had to leave the evening of the 9th. The positive was that he would now be home the evening of the 11th, so he could make my 40-week appointment on the 12th but had to leave again the afternoon of the 14th. The negative was for almost three weeks, I had been showing signs labor could start at any moment.

After this news, I did what I knew I needed to: move the emotions I felt through my body. I went for a walk. As the wave of emotions came over me, I shouted out loud through my tears as the realness set in my husband could miss the birth of our son. This thought devastated me to my core. The only fear I'd ever had about the birth could be coming true.

Then I heard my Guides deliver a message clear as day: "If everything went to plan, The Universe couldn't show off her magic. When you begin to show doubt, she reassures you that she's always been there, but she had to let you stand on your own." I immediately stopped, smiled with wet tears still on my face, took a deep, cleansing breath, and sighed it out. That message was exactly what I needed. That message at that moment reminded me yet again to surrender. I've always known there are higher guiding forces, but I needed the reminder that I was not in control. Whatever was going to happen, would happen, when it was supposed to.

After this, I settled into the waiting game, focusing on what I could control. I relaxed, gave myself Reiki, meditated, did hypnobirthing, nourished my body with healthy foods, and continued to connect my breath with movement, like yoga. My husband left on the 9th and on his arrival day to come home on the 11th, I dreamed of my son telling me again, "Go with the flow. I'm coming."

For my 40-week appointment on September 12th, I was already 3-4 cm dilated, and my cervix was thinning out to prepare for birth as I was 80% effaced. After sharing with my midwife our concerns about my husband's upcoming departure, she performed a membrane sweep in hopes of progressing labor along. We crossed our fingers but were along for the ride.

It was September 13th. My due date was finally here, and my husband was home 36 more hours before he had to leave again. The rollercoaster of emotions the past three weeks had taken its toll, but at this point, we both had settled into 'what was meant to be, would be,' mentality. We went to bed that night, still waiting for labor to start. My mucus plug had fallen out that afternoon, but still no movement.

I woke up at 1:15 am with some discomfort, but nothing unmanageable. Then, at 2:30 am on the dot, my water broke. Finally! I shouted in excitement for my husband to wake up and told him to call our doula and that I was going to shower. My doula, cool as a cucumber, instructed my husband to start timing my contractions for the next hour and to let her know my progress. While in the shower, the pain started to intensify, and it was harder to tell my husband when to start and stop the timer.

"If you're telling me right, your contractions are already 2-2.5 minutes apart!" He said unsurely. "I don't care what everyone else has told us. We need to grab our bag and get to the birthing center!" I screeched through labored breaths. I remained in the shower while my husband took our dog out and loaded the car.

At 3:11 am, we pulled out of the driveway and were on our way to the birthing center, our ETA being about an hour. He texted our doula to let her know we were en route. As he drove through the twists and turns of the backroads, I clenched the grab handle above the door and focused on my breathing as the contractions ensued.

As my laboring continued to intensify on our way to the birthing center, a car pulled out in front of us, going the perfect speed limit of 45 mph. "I need you to pass this car and get us there," I said through the wave of the current contraction. "Babe, we have plenty of time." He said calmly. "I do not want to have this baby in this car!" I shouted. "You're a professional race car driver! Pass this damn car!" Safety first, he waited until the center yellow line went from two solid stripes to dotted and passed the car, which was now going under the posted speed limit.

As we arrived at the birthing center, my doula and midwife greeted us in the parking lot. As soon as I got out of the car, I told my midwife I felt nauseous. "Yep, honey. That can happen." She responded calmly and politely. I immediately went over to the grass and vomited. "Imagine if he hadn't passed that car," I thought. "I would've gotten sick in the car!"

I waddled into the birthing center just after 4 a.m. and labored on the toilet while they filled the inflatable pool with warm, soothing water. Once I moved to the pool, I embodied everything I had visualized: calm and confident breaths, resting in a yogi squat in between the surges, even cheering on my supportive squad around me there, and making some jokes. The blissful birth I had envisioned repeatedly was coming to life.

As I was making my final pushes to bring my son earthside, I watched in the mirror they had placed in the water. Watching each push bring him closer to me, so I could finally hold him in my arms, gave me the power I needed to keep going. I held my husband's hand with my left hand and reached down with my right, and on the final push, I grabbed my son and guided him out of the water and into my arms. At 6:55 am, our son was born. I shouted with gleeful tears running down my face, "We did it!" I cried. I looked back at my husband; he looked at me, smiling, so proud of the beautiful, healthy son we brought into the world. The best part was we did it together. He was there to witness it all.

A few hours after giving birth, my son and I got a clean bill of health to check out and go home. Once arriving home, my husband got an hour of skin-to-skin and left for the airport.

If my husband's schedule hadn't changed, he would've left on the 13th. Since I went into labor in the middle of the night, he wouldn't have been able to get a flight home in time, and he would've missed the birth. "Go with the flow. I'm coming" was how it all played out. My son was right all along.

My Son was born on September 14, 2023, exactly a year to the day I sat in the Birthing Cave in Sedona and welcomed a soul into my womb. This experience always serves as a reminder of how we can create magic in our lives. Be open to surrendering and blindly following the crumbs along the path, unsure where it will lead you, but knowing it will be something greater than you could have ever imagined.

Using intuition, which enhanced my telepathic communication with my son, is a gift we are all innately born with. You just have to tap into it.

CHAPTER 12

Mama's Intuition

Albert Einstein said, "The only real valuable thing is intuition," and I wholeheartedly agree. There's nothing more substantial than a Mama's intuition. Since the dawn of humanity, mothers have had an innate ability to sense when their child is in danger or when something feels 'off.' Scientifically, this wonder has been called 'microchimerism.' This phenomenon happens due to the presence of small cells that have been transferred from one individual to another. During pregnancy, not only is the placenta carrying nutrients from the mother to her baby, but we have now discovered that the baby's DNA also transfers to the mother, establishing a biological life-long bond between the two. I believe this genetic miracle only amplifies the magic within a mother's intuition to connect with her child, echoing what I shared in the last chapter.

As a new mom, my instincts faced several tests. The first instance occurred when my son was only seven weeks old. I noticed his typically sweet and calm demeanor shifting to one of agitation. Just a few days later, he began exhibiting signs of congestion.

Our eight-week check-up was scheduled with our pediatrician for the following week. I contacted him to see if we could have the appointment sooner to investigate my son's condition. We were set to be seen the next Monday. During the visit, the pediatrician reassured me that my son appeared fine and only had a cold. Despite my instincts suggesting otherwise, I questioned whether I was overreacting as a first-time mom. That night, while feeding him, he seemed to have more difficulty breathing. Watching his chest rise and fall with each breath, I thought, "Something isn't right," but then reminded myself, "We just saw the pediatrician, and he said he was fine, only a cold. It's normal for him to catch several colds this first year as his immune system develops."

On Tuesday morning, when my husband woke up beside me, I shared what I had seen during the night feedings and expressed my ongoing worries about our son. He comforted me and reminded me that the pediatrician had just diagnosed it as a cold.

We kept administering saline for his sinuses and used the nozebot to remove the mucus from his nose in hopes of easing his discomfort so he could continue to eat. I stood with him in the shower several times during the day, talking to him and his body. As the water ran down his little body, I called on Reiki to fill the shower. While giving him Reiki, I would tell his body it was 'strong and vibrant.' I told his body it was doing what it was designed to: fight off whatever pathogen it contracted and not be scared. Whatever this was, it would only strengthen his immune system.

As the day progressed, I sensed again that something wasn't right. The thought of it being "just a cold" didn't sit well with me. I decided to send a video to my doula, who I had come to know as a good friend, to get her insight. As a mother of three, she confirmed my concerns, stating that it seemed more serious than a cold, and advised me to keep an eye on his symptoms. I spent most of the night by his side, feeling uneasy as I watched him sleep. I noticed his breathing becoming more labored and distinct wheezing sounds emerging.

On Wednesday morning, I told my husband that regardless of what the pediatrician had said, we needed another appointment. I knew something was off. With RSV season upon us, I was increasingly concerned that my son might have it. My husband watched our son breathe and he agreed I needed to contact our pediatrician for a follow-up. Unfortunately, he was out of town for a conference, so I sent him a video. He acknowledged that my son's breathing seemed labored and suggested we seek pediatric urgent care in his absence. My husband then remembered that the birthing center recently opened a pediatric clinic. Fortunately, they could see us right away.

The new pediatrician happened to be one of the midwives that we adored. Concerned it might be RSV, she met us in the parking lot alongside the nurse from my prenatal visits, who was also wonderful. With care, the pediatrician checked his breathing and reassured us that his lungs were clear, which eased our worries since we had heard unsettling stories about babies being hospitalized for RSV. She took a swab from his tiny nose and informed us we would receive the results the following day. That night, I settled into the recliner and gave skin-to-skin as my son slept upright on my chest, hoping to make it easier for him to breathe.

The next day, the pediatrician from the birthing center called me to confirm what my gut had known all along. It wasn't just a cold. My son tested positive for RSV. Fortunately for us, no intervention was needed. I continued with lots of skin-to-skin contact to produce oxytocin and breastfed him every two hours. Nature is impressive; when your child is sick, your body automatically produces the antibodies your baby needs to heal.

After several days filled with cuddles, kisses, and relaxing Reiki sessions, my son showed signs of improvement. However, during this period, his stools transitioned from yellow and seedy to green. Worried about this change, I reached out to our primary pediatrician again. He reassured me that it's common for babies' stool colors to vary, emphasizing that green is normal. Despite this, I still felt uneasy. I began to worry that I was a hypochondriac first-time mom, overreacting to everything, but to my credit, my instincts had proven correct just the week before.

I let a few more days go by, and the green got progressively worse and slimy. "Something is off," I thought to myself… again. I reached out to my doula, and she responded immediately, "Oh yeah. That's a food sensitivity." That day, I scheduled an appointment with a naturopathic doctor who offered muscle testing. If you're unfamiliar, muscle testing, also known as applied kinesiology, is an alternative medicine practice from the basic idea of Sir Issac Newton's Law of Motion, "For every action in nature there is an equal and opposite reaction." In this case, it means that muscle weakness is induced by any internal disruptions your body is experiencing.

We were seen just two days later, and at the appointment, I was the surrogate for my son. As I held him in my lap, the doctor tested my auric field first, then my son's. After this, she grabbed bins of vials to test what my son may be sensitive to. There were common ones, such as eggs and peanuts, that she wanted to test first. I then raised my right arm straight out in front of me for the doctor to evaluate. She performed the "test" by holding the vial with the potentially sensitive ingredient behind my ear and gently pressing on my arm with her other hand, testing the muscle strength. If the muscle feels weaker than when she tested my field in the beginning, and my arm gives way, then she knows there is a sensitivity for my son. Remember, I'm the surrogate.

The two main sensitivities were dairy and cruciferous vegetables, which I was eating like it was my job. Broccoli, cauliflower, and kale; I ate cruciferous vegetables multiple times daily. I wasn't consuming much dairy, but this seemed to be the icing on the cake, considering how many veggies I ate.

Since I was breastfeeding, I had to eliminate consuming what he was sensitive to. After just a week of eradicating the foods my son tested sensitive to, his stools returned to "normal," what I deemed "normal" and what had been his "normal."

In less than three weeks, I had been made out to be an overreacting, worried first-time mom by a medical professional. However, I refused to let their skepticism shake my instincts. I trusted my intuition and continued to follow what felt right. In both instances, I was correct, not the doctor. While I do believe it's important to listen to your doctor's advice, remember that you know your child better than anyone else. Trust your instincts, and don't allow others to sway you from what you believe is best for your child.

Trusting your intuition during pregnancy is just as important for you as it is for your unborn baby. When Jean found out she was pregnant, she was ecstatic. One day, 10 years before this discovery, she had been walking through Marshall's and came across a brown and white polka dot blanket. She was quite fond of polka dots, and while rubbing it between her hands, she heard plain as day, "You are going to have a son." She looked around, and no one was nearby. Having often 'heard' things throughout her life that always came to be, she purchased the blanket and couldn't wait to tell her husband.

They already had an amazing daughter and had been discussing wanting another baby. Jean showed her husband, Will, the blanket and then proclaimed that God told her they would have a son. He smiled at her and just shook his head as he always did when she declared these things. He was unsure of how she received these messages or even who she was hearing but knew better than to doubt her.

Most women who have decided to conceive can attest that the only thing that matches the excitement of possibility is the stress of the unknown. Am I ovulating? Will I be late? Am I pregnant? How long to wait to take a test? So many questions and so many variables. Jean was no exception to this. When months turned to years with no successful pregnancy, she decided to look for answers.

First, there were hormonal checks by the obstetrician. The results were devastating as they indicated she was not ovulating and, therefore, could not get pregnant. Jean knew she would have a son even if she didn't know how. Next, she was sent to a fertility specialist clinic. There, it was discovered that she was ovulating, just not on a normal schedule. After some more invasive tests, it appeared that one of her fallopian tubes was blocked. This had a potential for repair, and Jean scheduled surgery. Hopeful that this was the answer, the procedure was performed, and the blocks were removed. At the follow-up, the doctor explained that everything was in natural working order now and pregnancy should be obtainable. If only it were that easy.

As more time passed with no viable pregnancy, IUI (intrauterine insemination) and IVF were discussed. Jean took time to evaluate what would be best for her and her body. Ultimately, she decided if she was meant to have a son, he would come the old-fashioned way. As years went by, the repeated disappointments drained Will's hope. They shifted their focus in life, and the blanket was eventually stored away. Although Jean struggled to comprehend, she maintained her faith and responded to her intuition and what she 'heard.'

At their first appointment after the positive pregnancy test, the obstetrician told them not to get attached to this pregnancy and not to tell anyone as it would not prove viable. This was due to Jean having suffered extensive full body and head trauma in a car accident just a couple of years earlier. The degree of the injuries to her pelvis and her brain led doctors to believe that she would not be able to grow or carry a fetus successfully. However, one night, after being cozy with her husband, Jean heard, 'That was the baby maker.' She smiled. She was familiar with that voice and knew what it meant. While Jean did not share the news as advised by her doctors, she knew this was the son she was told about years ago while standing in Marshall's with the polka-dot blanket.

Jean was in her second trimester when she told the OB that she couldn't possibly conceal her very evident change in body shape any longer. Around week 21, the doctor informed her that the baby now had a fighting chance at life outside the womb, so she should carry it as long as she could, and they would be able to 'get the baby out.' Caesarean was discussed, but Jean was not comfortable with that idea, nor with going through that sort of recovery if it could be avoided, as she was still in physical therapy from the car accident. As she sought guidance through prayer and meditation on what would be best for her and her son, she was reassured that she would be able to deliver him.

Jean's pregnancy was labeled high-risk due to her age and past injuries, resulting in frequent doctor appointments. During her checkup at 35 weeks, she informed the OB on duty about her headache and unusual vision. Although Jean felt unwell, she couldn't pinpoint the cause. Her blood pressure showed slight elevation, but tests revealed everything was normal. The doctor advised her to rest. While Jean suspected something was off, she attributed it to lack of sleep. With the baby already considered 'big,' the pressure it exerted on her unstable pelvis resulted in significant pain, interfering with her sleep. Her next appointment was scheduled just four days later, on Monday of the following week, so she planned to rest beforehand.

The weekend brought an increase in headache intensity and a decline in her vision. By her appointment on Monday, Jean knew she needed to express concern again, but to the current OB working that day. The OB advised Jean to have blood work done at the hospital rather than in the office so she would receive the results immediately. She also wanted Jean's blood pressure monitored while she waited. Jean inquired as to how long this would take since "she had a list of things to do today, and the hospital wasn't on it." The OB reassured her it would only take about an hour, but it was the best course of action.

After arriving at the hospital and having labs drawn, Jean was placed in a bed where they could monitor her blood pressure. They turned the lights down and told her to rest while they waited to hear from the doctor. Jean tried to rest, but the repeated alarms in the hallway kept waking her. About 30 minutes later, a nurse came in to check on her and asked about the status of her headache and whether she would like some Tylenol. Normally Jean didn't take medicine unless it was necessary, but the headache had become too much to bear, and she welcomed the Tylenol. The nurse left, and a few minutes later, a different nurse popped in with the meds in hand.

This nurse had short blonde hair, a big, warm smile, and the energy of a fairy. She patted Jean on the leg and informed her she would now be her nurse and was taking her to her room. Jean sat up, confused, and explained that she had a to-do list for today and that this was only supposed to take an hour. The nurse responded with a calming yet authoritative voice, "Oh honey, you're not leaving the hospital until you have a baby," and proceeded to wheel Jean down the hall of the hospital to the maternity wing. Apparently, the alarms that kept waking her were from her blood pressure monitor, indicating she was in a hypertensive crisis.

Jean was experiencing preeclampsia, a condition marked by high blood pressure during pregnancy, posing significant risks to both mother and child. The headaches, blurred vision, and protein in urine were all due to this condition. Preeclampsia can also cause seizures for which Jean was now at risk. For the baby, this condition can result in inadequate oxygen and nutrient supply, potentially causing delayed development, preterm birth, and other serious complications. The risks associated preeclampsia emphasized the urgent need for delivery.

As the on-call obstetrician discussed the situation, Jean closed her eyes and took some deep breaths to allow the confusion and panic she was experiencing to settle. She found herself at ease again. "I am going to deliver my son," she responded when the doctor said he would be meeting with the high-risk team to establish a plan of action and timeline for the caesarean. At 36 weeks, the unborn baby is still considered premature. As such, they often like to administer a steroid to help with fetal lung development, but that needs time to be effective. Jean 'heard' that her son 'didn't need it' and told the doctor she did not want it. He noted the request in her file and said that, in all reality, there probably wasn't enough time for it to be effective before the baby's arrival. Being in a hypertensive crisis means time is of the essence for the health and safety of both mother and baby. The doctor said he would take Jean's request for a vaginal delivery attempt to the team and see what they say.

He came back about an hour later and informed Jean that they would offer her a small window of time to see if an internal balloon could help shift her pelvis. This process would be quite uncomfortable, and even if her pelvis moved the way it needed to, it did not guarantee a caesarean wouldn't be necessary. Jean understood and agreed that if the deadline came, then she would have the caesarean, but she knew she had to try. She had been told she would have a son; she would have a viable pregnancy; her headaches weren't just from lack of sleep; she would deliver him on her own. She listened to her intuition every step of the way, and she wasn't going to stop now.

Twelve hours later, the balloon was removed in the wee hours of the morning. Her pelvis had shifted, and they could start the medication to induce labor. They had given Jean antiseizure medication upon arriving on the unit along with medicine to help her blood pressure protocol for preeclampsia. At this point, she was not in crisis mode but was still having elevated blood pressure, and the deadline to have her baby was still in place. Jean, though exhausted, knew everything was going to be just fine.

When Jean dilated to 10cm, the nurse told her she would get the doctor and NICU staff ready for his arrival. Ten minutes after the doctor told her to push, a healthy baby boy was born with the 'strongest set of lungs' on the unit and weighing nearly 7 pounds.

Jean went into this birth experience with the confidence to trust her intuition and her body. It was the emotional scars from her first birth experience that had given her that strength. Having been repeatedly dismissed because she was 'only 22' and her concerns being chalked up to being a 'new mom that didn't know better' taught her to trust the guidance given to her from the voice she 'heard,' to speak up for her concerns and needs confidently, and to find peace even in the seemingly dark days of it all.

Mothers have told me countless stories about feeling ostracized by others, but they stood their ground and advocated for themselves and their babies. Their intuition never failed them, and yours won't either.

Intuitive Gifts

We are all born with intuitive gifts, but due to us usually living in a state of survival and keeping up with daily tasks and responsibilities, we've lost sight of how powerful our innate gifts really are. There are common ways you may have unconsciously connected with your intuition.

Think of a time you had a gut feeling not to take your usual route to work or destination, and you chose a different route, later to find out there was an accident on the road you avoided. What about when you knew a situation was going to work out in your favor, and those around you doubted a positive outcome? Or, have you heard an internal voice at times give you advice that feels like you but not quite you? Have you seen things happen before they do? I know for certain at least one, if not more, of these questions above resonates with you.

What I just described are the main intuitive "clairs." Clairsentient is when you have a feeling, a physical reaction. In the example above, it was a gut feeling not to take your usual route, later finding out there was an accident. During Reiki sessions, I frequently connect with this clair when I feel a physical sensation in my body that wasn't there before I started working with a client. For instance, if I begin to feel pressure in my head while working with someone, this sensation indicates that the client has been experiencing some discomfort in their head, usually a headache.

Claircognizant refers to having an innate knowing. These messages are like a lightbulb going off in my brain as if someone has opened my head and inserted the thought into my mind. For example, I might experience an immediate distrust toward someone I just met without any concrete evidence to justify it. Yet, six months later, their true nature reveals what I sensed from the beginning.

Clairaudient is when you hear certain information being communicated to you. I receive messages from my Guides and the Angels I work with. It's a distinctive difference from my inner voice. At times, I'll ask for guidance while remaining receptive to incoming messages. I often utilize my clairaudience during sessions, where my clients' guides provide messages that I share. Occasionally, songs may come to me that seem irrelevant at the time but later reveal a deep meaning for the client upon reflection.

Clairvoyance is a French word for 'clear seeing.' Clairvoyants work with their Third Eye chakra to 'see' symbols, colors, actual images, or even a scene being played like a movie in their mind. In my practice and working with clients, I have found that this clair is the most common and easiest to develop for someone rekindling their relationship with their intuition.

Having elaborated on those, how do they resonate with you? Often, one or two clairs stand out, and it's perfectly fine if only one is your gift. While I relate to all the clairs, I find clairvoyance and clairaudience come most naturally to me. After completing my Reiki trainings, I enhanced my claircognizant and clairsentient abilities, and I now utilize all four depending on the situation.

How to Deepen Your Intuition

Babies, unfortunately, don't come with data, graphs, and a manual. (Wouldn't that be nice!) Your strongest guide is to lean on your motherly intuition. Your baby will communicate its needs with you. Over thousands of years, nature has perfected the incredible intuitiveness, your intuitiveness, of what the mother needs to do to care for her baby.

Just as certain sports, playing an instrument(s), or being a natural artist comes effortlessly for some, others must invest more time in practice and studying the said art. Maybe you're one that these intuitive gifts come with ease, perhaps you've already put in some work to connect with your abilities, or maybe this is all new to you, and you are interested but are unsure where to start.

Regardless of your current stage, honing your intuition is similar to training a muscle for strength; your abilities also need consistent effort to flourish. You must dedicate yourself to showing up, putting in the effort, and practicing to enhance your intuitive capabilities. If this is your first time exploring this topic, it's natural to feel both excited and a bit overwhelmed, that's perfectly normal. I will provide exercises to help you begin or to reconnect with your intuitive gifts. For those who have already been utilizing their intuitive skills, excellent! You may find these tools below as a refresher or discover new ways to enrich your practice.

Asking for Signs

Over ten years ago, when I first began learning about working with my Guides and Angels, I must admit, it seemed a little outlandish. That was until it wasn't.

During a flight to California with my husband, I became immersed in the book 'How to Meet and Work with Spirit Guides' by Ted Andrews. I was captivated by its content and continued reading even when it was time to prepare for bed. Among the suggestions was to ask your Guide for a sign, and the first thing that came to my mind was a white feather. Before falling asleep that night, I distinctly remember stating, "If this is real, if you truly exist, I am asking you to give me a sign of a white feather before we leave California. Since we are at the beach, I don't want the feather to be on the beach because that would seem too easy since there are birds around. Instead, I want this feather to appear in the most inconspicuous place."

The next morning, I felt groggy after staying up too late reading, having only managed a few hours of sleep. As my husband and I headed downstairs for breakfast, he walked ahead of me. When I turned to close the door to our room, he exclaimed, "Wow. Where did all these feathers come from?" I glanced back to see what he meant, and chills ran down my spine. The hotel hallway was filled with a multitude of white feathers. My expression must have given everything away, as my husband looked at me with concern and asked, "What's wrong?" I replied, "You won't believe this." I explained, "Last night, I couldn't put down the book on connecting with Spirit Guides, and it said to ask them for a sign, so I did. Before bed I asked for them to show me a white feather as a sign. They clearly were over achievers on this." The look on his face was in disbelief, too. I couldn't tell if he was suspicious about what I was becoming interested in, the story I told him about me asking for the sign and he being there to witness it, or all the above.

This was the first time my spirit team communicated with me, and I've been working with them ever since. What I cherish most about this relationship is their constant gift of feathers, including white ones. While my husband and I were taking our pregnancy announcement photos, I spotted a single white feather beside me. I smiled, picked it up, and shared this story with our photographer. She captured a picture of the white feather alongside our ultrasound photo. It's one of my favorites, reminding me that my spirit team always supports me.

For you, your spirit team may be God or whoever you call on as Source. It may be a loved one who has passed and whom you believe is looking after you. Whoever your team is, they are ready to support you. All you have to do is call on them.

Journaling

Journaling has endless benefits and is another excellent way to strengthen your intuition. I encourage you to write down anything and everything that comes to you. I found my Guides and Angels were communicating with me in my dreams before I fully developed the confidence to connect with them while awake.

Before going to bed, I would call on them to deliver any messages I needed to receive while in my sleep. When waking up, I would write down everything I could remember. Over time, I would re-read what I had written and be amazed at what came through. Sometimes, they were very directive on a path I needed to go, or I would dream about a particular person who ended up playing an integral part in the next step I needed to take to get me where I was looking to go. I would pay attention to patterns or look into the deeper meaning of what a dream meant.

A common theme in my dreams at one point was snakes. Due to my fear of snakes, I believed they were nightmares. After writing down these repeated dreams, I reflected on their deeper meaning.

Dreaming of snakes symbolizes transformation due to their ability to shed skin. This reflects the process of letting go of outdated habits and beliefs. In my waking life, I was dedicated to improving my health, both physically and emotionally. Additionally, since snakes consume their prey whole, these dreams can signify a thirst for knowledge, which I was actively pursuing at that time, as these dreams kept recurring. They reassured me that I was on the right path in my waking life and highlighted that there was nothing to fear. Ultimately, they confirmed that I was supported in following my passions.

When I've taught others to tap into their intuitive gifts, I've encouraged them to journal what comes through. Nothing was off the table; they would write it down no matter how silly it seemed. Some chose to meditate and would write down what they saw, felt, heard, or had a gut feeling about; others felt automatic writing was a better way for them to connect. As their hand freely wrote, their conscious mind let go, allowing space for their gifts to shine. The best part was when these students took the time to reflect on what they had written; many things that seemed like just an idea or an image had actually transpired. This gave them the confidence boost they needed and proved they were intuitive. It had just been dormant and needed to be re-awakened.

Meditation

Meditation has proven benefits for the mind, body, and mood, but it is also an excellent way to sharpen your intuitive gifts. Learning to quiet the noise around and within you allows you to be receptive to messages coming through from your Guides, Angels, or Source. As you learned in the mindfulness chapter, there are many ways to meditate, so choose what fits you best, and know how you choose to meditate can fluctuate depending on where you are in your practice or potential location.

Albert Einstein took meditation breaks throughout the day to develop new theories. He said, "Through meditation, I found answers before I even asked the question." Was Einstein receiving messages from a Source, or was he tapping into this infinite wisdom by quieting the mind?

When you commit to frequent meditation, you become familiar with your mind's everyday landscape. The purpose is to stall the chatter of the monkey-mind that is always racing. As you focus on the breath, set the ego aside, and release attachment to what may be revealed, you will notice insights that expose themselves. You may see a pink rose, you may hear a message given to you, you may feel a new sensation in your body as your body communicates with you while you're in stillness, or you may have the knowing you need to apply for that job that you've been avoiding. The purpose here is to have an open mind and heart and let things flow naturally.

I've worked with many clients who are addicted to chaos, so the thought of meditation frightens them. They become fearful of what may show up when sitting down in silence. If you believe you may be afraid to meditate due to the same fear, a walking meditation may be a comfortable place to start. Remember to free yourself from distractions during this time, such as listening to music or a podcast. Become one with nature and enjoy the present moment.

Ujjay Breath

You previously learned how to perform the Ujjay breath, or what's also known as "Ocean breathing." To perform, with your mouth closed, you inhale through the nose, creating space in the back of your throat, breathing deep into the belly, and feeling your diaphragm expand. Keep your mouth closed and jaw relaxed, and exhale through the nose, continuing space in the back of the throat. As you exhale, notice your breath becoming audible. The Ujjay breath is not only a wonderful mindfulness technique, but it is also an excellent tool for activating your intuition. Not only does it calm the nervous system, which helps you enter a meditative state, but it also stimulates the hypothalamus. The hypothalamus is a part of the brain near the pituitary gland, and it is known as the part of the brain that heightens awareness. When our awareness is heightened, this leads to our intuition opening up. This impactful breathing technique can boost your meditation practice, amplifying your intuitive gifts.

Your intuition is your real-life superpower that you can call on anytime. Strengthening your intuition will help you communicate with your baby telepathically when they are in the womb and connect with them once they are earthside. Eventually, your mind will take a backseat, allowing your intuition to guide all your decisions and become your compass. Trust your motherly instincts; they will never steer you wrong, and this certainly goes for when you're giving birth.

CHAPTER 13

Birth

I viewed my birth as training for the biggest event of my life, as if I were going to the Olympics. It was me and my son's time to shine. Each day, I concentrated on what I could influence: the preparation for the birth while relinquishing control of the final outcome and accepting what would be.

In the 'Mindful Mama' chapter, I described my mental preparation. I journaled to my son, recited positive affirmations out loud, and engaged in daily physical activity, walking 10-15 miles weekly, practicing yoga with breathwork 2-3 times a week to ready myself for labor, and strength training to build endurance for delivery and birth. Additionally, before bed, I focused extensively on meditation and visualization of how I envisioned my birth experience, programming my subconscious mind.

I kept my eyes on my paper and maintained my circle of my good vibe tribe, safeguarding and preserving my energy body. I was thoroughly engrossed in my 'training' plan, and everything was intentional and purposeful, especially when prioritizing rest in the final weeks leading up to the big day.

When it was showtime, I can confidently say I had no fear. I trusted my body would do what it was designed to do. If my plan became deviated and medical intervention was needed, I had faith in the team of people I had surrounded myself with to do what was necessary and safe for my son and me.

Upon reaching the birthing center and entering the warm, soothing birthing pool, I immersed myself in everything I had prepared for. My calming, deep breaths felt instinctual as I flowed into the yoga postures I had practiced for seven months leading up to this moment. In a meditative state, I synchronized with my body, embracing each contraction with gratitude, knowing each one brought me closer to holding my son for the very first time. I connected with him telepathically, expressing my readiness and embracing the unfolding of our birth story. Throughout my journey, I had felt the support of higher guiding forces, and I was confident this moment would prove the same.

As first-time mothers typically labor between 12 to 24 hours before giving birth, I mentally prepared for that timeframe. However, my water broke at 2:30 am, and I delivered at 6:55 am. I believe my preparations throughout my pregnancy significantly contributed to this quicker process.

Research indicates that over 75% of first-time mothers deliver over a week past their due date. I can't help but wonder if this is linked to the anxieties that many women face as they become mothers. Do they feel unprepared as they approach childbirth? Is it fear because it's something new to experience? Is it her life is getting ready to change forever, and she is unsure of what motherhood will look like for her? Or, could it be the shedding of her old self as she transforms into the new version of herself?

Holding onto fear generates stress and anxiety in your body. This stress triggers the release of cortisol, which can hinder the progression of labor, potentially delaying your body's natural response to initiate it. Furthermore, stress leads to muscle tension, heightening your pain perception during labor.

In contrast, oxytocin is crucial for contractions; higher levels of oxytocin can lead to a quicker labor. Therefore, focusing on breathwork, visualization, and positive affirmations, while expressing gratitude for your body's efforts for you and your baby, can support you in reaching the moment of holding your baby for the first time.

Birth Plan

As you're closing in on the big day of welcoming your baby, having your birth plan in place will set your mind at ease, and as you now know, when your mind is at peace, your body will follow in its footsteps.

A few birthing strategy topics you may want to consider include: what plans are in place if you should go into labor sooner than your due date? Who will attend your birth with you, if anyone? How is your support system, good vibe tribe, in place to promote a positive birthing experience induced with encouragement and comfort? Who will advocate for what you want in case you're unable to? Do you want to allow any visitors, and, of course, who will deliver your sushi tray to you after birth?

Tailoring your birth experience to align with your personality will help you feel safe, which will help create a calm and stress-free atmosphere. If the mere idea of a hospital makes your blood pressure spike, discuss the possibility of a birthing center or home birth with your trusted healthcare team. If those alternatives aren't feasible or compatible, inquire about adjustments to make your hospital experience more comfortable. For instance, can the lights be dimmed and music played? What kind of music do you prefer—soothing, upbeat, or a mix? Will your partner and supportive individuals be allowed in the room? Is it possible to use essential oil diffusers? Compile a list of what helps you relax and share it with your doctor or midwife.

The same is applicable if you are slated to give birth at home or a birthing center. Communicate with your providers what's important to include in your experience to encourage a relaxing and comfortable environment. Also, depending on your background and experiences, touch may be uncomfortable for you and cause tension instead of relaxation. If this pertains to you, expressing this beforehand will bring more peace to your birth experience.

What creates fear and anxiety is the unknown, so educating yourself on the array of potential birthing possibilities is key to setting yourself up for mental success. For example, if your plan is a vaginal delivery, I'd encourage you to inform yourself about the protocols of a cesarean section. This is not to distract you from your ideal birth but will help set your mind at ease if you should need one. Understanding the process will alleviate your anxiety around the unknown. Sometimes, your plans may change, and that's okay, but it's how you handle and work through these adversities, and after that, that matters.

If unexpected complications arise, whether a new procedure is suggested or intervention is required, you have the right to ask questions. Your provider should deliver clear, unbiased answers to help you make informed decisions regarding your and your baby's well-being. They must also share evidence-based information, along with the potential risks and benefits of the new options available. If you feel uneasy about the choices presented, inquire about additional alternatives. If no other options exist, consider, "Which choice aligns most closely with my ideal birth?" If it's not an emergency and you have time to talk with your partner or doula, you can request that the nurse, doctor, or midwife leave the room, allowing you to make a confident and informed decision. Trust your instincts about what's best and lean on your doula or support partner who understands your birth plan. Ensure you give full consent before allowing your provider to proceed. Be clear and assertive about your wishes. You're the boss of your body; your voice needs to be heard, your concerns addressed, and your decisions respected.

As you follow the birthing path, whether as planned or unplanned, that will welcome your baby into the world safely, focus your attention on what you've trained for: breathing, visualizations, positive affirmations, and all things that will keep your mind and body as relaxed as possible.

Ensure your support team has a list of your intentional affirmations you'd like incorporated so they can help you recite them throughout your experience. Some you may wish to use are, "We've got this." "My body was designed for this." "We are healthy, we are strong, we are vibrant." "This isn't hard, it's just new." "I'm ready for you." For a full list of intentional affirmations you may like to use, visit www.melbraun.com.

If you have certain breathwork techniques you've been practicing, also give them to your supporter(s) and have them remind you to connect with your breath throughout labor and delivery. (A bonus is your supporter is already familiar with these, so they are second nature to them just as they are for you.) Breathwork is a powerful compliment to your laboring and birth experience as it will help your muscles and mind relax, making your birth process easier and reducing pain. It also brings you and your baby more oxygen, giving you more energy and strength, and can help reduce tearing.

No matter how you plan to give birth, talk through positions for labor and birth with your support team and incorporate those positions in your 'training' at home. For me, getting into a 'yogi squat' was a place of relaxation for my mind and body and served as a reminder to concentrate on my breath. In between contractions throughout my labor, this was my go-to position. The familiarity also brought comfort in a new situation for me, like labor. It kept me present, focusing on what I knew, allowing me to surrender to whatever was next.

No matter how you bring life into this world, it's a beautiful and empowering experience. Giving birth shines light on your incredible capabilities and reminds you how magical you are. Only you possess the ability to grow life within you and give birth. Without you, humanity would face extinction. That's truly remarkable and deserves recognition.

To end your birth plan on a high note, plan who will capture these once-in-a-lifetime moments. Decide if you want pictures and videos taken during labor, birth, and/or after. Time will be a blur, and you will enjoy looking back on this meaningful occasion as you welcomed life into the world.

Hospital Bag

Everyone has heard about the hospital bag, that you should have ready around the beginning of your third trimester, but what should go in it?

After finalizing your birth plan, which the information above should have helped clarify, print a few copies to take with you. One can be given to your provider, another can be added to your chart for the nurses to review, and you might also post a copy in your room. If there are important points in your birthing plan, consider highlighting them for easy reference.

Chargers. This includes phones, tablets, and portable speaker. Also, chargers with longer cables can be helpful in case the electrical outlet is further away from the bed. Extra tip, if you plan to create a birthing playlist, ensure you have more than 20 songs. Labor can take some time, and you don't want to listen to the same songs repeatedly. (Or, maybe you do. Who am I to judge?)

If you can use essential oils at your birthing facility and they aren't provided, make sure to bring your own diffuser and oils. Consider including lavender, which encourages relaxation and can help alleviate nausea, along with lemon, ginger, and peppermint oils. Both peppermint and ginger can also be effective for headaches, which has the possibility to occur. I personally keep peppermint beadlets in my purse for those moments when my stomach feels off or I experience headaches; they always help. Ylang Ylang is beneficial for easing anxiety and relieving pain and muscle tension. Incorporating oils as your partner massages you during birth is another wonderful idea, and if they know Reiki they can give you and your baby Reiki as you're laboring, and while giving birth. Additionally, I always have eucalyptus on hand at home, as it pairs wonderfully with lavender to create a spa-like atmosphere, which is especially calming during labor. Using essential oils postpartum can also improve your sleep, which is essential for recovery.

Pillows. If you've never used a hospital pillow, a pancake is thicker than they are. These pillows can be quite uncomfortable, so I suggest bringing your and your partner's pillow from home. If you plan to breastfeed, I'd also suggest packing a nursing pillow. I highly recommend the Brest Friend Nursing Pillow. It's flat and firm cushion is great for supportive breastfeeding. If you're spending a few days in the hospital, bringing your own towels may be a nice touch too.

Having your toiletries available to freshen up will feel extra luxurious post birth. These items may include but are not limited to, body wash, shampoo/ conditioner, hairbrush and hair ties, toothbrush and toothpaste, deodorant, lotion, and lip balm. If you wear glasses, bring your case so they are in a safe place. Or, if you wear contacts, bring extra contact lenses, the case, and contact solution.

Comfortable clothing is essential after delivery, regardless of how you give birth. When selecting your attire, avoid anything restrictive. Even after a vaginal delivery, you will still feel some soreness. I strongly recommend a comfortable top that provides easy access for breastfeeding and/or skin-to-skin contact. For bottoms, loose, lightweight sleep pants are an excellent choice. Regarding bras, it's a matter of personal preference, so I'll leave that one up to you on what you think will be most comfortable. If you're planning a water birth, consider bringing two bras: a black one for the water and another for after the birth. Cozy socks are another great addition to your bag; you might opt for those with grips underneath, and you might want to pack slippers. You may have some swelling when you're released to head home, so bring easy slip-on shoes. Finally, a robe can complete your comfortable postpartum ensemble.

Having your postpartum care kit packed in your bag is a must. The hospital will provide pads and mesh underwear, but you may prefer postpartum underwear from FridaMom or something similar. Some mothers have said that Depends felt more secure and comfortable for them. Use what suits you best. I didn't use perineal spray since I barely tore, but I know other moms who found it invaluable. It's wise to have it readily available just in case. Another must-have is a peri bottle, which helps clean and soothe your perineal area post-birth. If you're planning to breastfeed, adding nipple cream to your bag is a great idea. I personally use coconut oil for many purposes (I'll elaborate on this in the next chapter), and it worked wonderfully for my sore nipples. You might also want to consider packing two types of nipple shields. Silver shields are known for their healing properties, and if you have smaller nipples, a nipple shield can help your baby latch better during breastfeeding.

Maybe the most important item for your bag is your nutrition. Have a reusable water bottle. Laboring exerts a lot of energy, and staying hydrated is a priority. I'd also encourage you to add electrolytes, whether this is a powder form to add to your water, or something like coconut water. Hammer nutrition energy gels can also be quick to eat to help give you the boost you need during labor. Snacks are great to add to your bag, and ones that are higher in protein are a bonus since the protein will help keep you fuller, longer. Think of protein bars, nuts, and jerky sticks. Or maybe you'd prefer veggie sticks like celery or carrot. Whatever snack you think will be appealing to you is what I'd suggest including. And the food I would put emphasis on is your post-birth Magic Mama Meals. Supplying your body with proper nutrients right away will only benefit you and your baby. You can certainly enjoy this alongside the sushi you've been craving, or serve it as a meal before or after you indulge in all the sushi rolls your heart desires.

Now that your bag is packed, let's discuss what your baby needs. Their list is quite a bit shorter. Thank goodness! Right?

Your baby's car seat should already be installed. Most car seats today come with a base, so you'll leave the base in the car and dislocate the car seat when it's time to bring your baby home. Don't be surprised if they supervise you strapping your child in for the first time to ensure you know how to secure them correctly, and they may even watch you click their car seat back into the base before leaving. Always put safety first with our precious cargo!

Everyone's favorite item to pack is your baby's going-home outfit. You may also want to pack two different outfits (newborn and 0-3 months) since you don't know how big your baby will be until they are born. If you choose to only pack one, a gown that ties at the bottom may be a nice option. Make sure to have a swaddle blanket as well. One will likely be provided by the birthing facility, but yours will be much softer. Also, don't be shy about asking a provider to show you how to swaddle your baby. A hat, mittens, and socks may also be something you'd like to include in your bag for your baby.

Having your pediatrician's information available will be helpful as your nurse will ask for it so they can easily forward your baby's medical records. Make sure to have your pediatrician's name, number, email address, and physical address for your birth facility's paperwork.

If you're planning to breastfeed and use a breast pump, it's essential to get accurately measured for your flange size. Often, the sizes provided are too large, preventing a proper fit and negatively impacting suction, which means you won't pump as much milk. You can ask your lactation consultant or your doula for sizing assistance. If you don't have someone to help, you can order a flange sizing kit online, such as Amazon, which includes a nipple ruler and various flange size options. You may decide not to take the breast pump into the hospital with you because of its size, but you may want to have it in your car, just in case you should need it after delivery. I'd also include a few breast milk storage bags as well.

If you decide not to breastfeed, remember to pack bottles and formula. A few insights: my son was born with a slightly retracted jaw due to being deep in my pelvis for an extended period. As a result, while in utero, he didn't rest his tongue on the roof of his mouth, leading to a highly arched palate. This made it challenging for him to use standard bottle nipples. If your baby struggles with bottles, I recommend trying a nipple that is flat on one side; the Nuk brand worked brilliantly for us. When selecting a formula, the options can feel overwhelming. If possible, opt for a brand that doesn't contain palm oil, as it can cause digestive issues and discomfort in babies. If your baby still seems unsettled, many babies have a dairy sensitivity until around six months, once their stomach has developed more. If you find yourself in this situation, there are other formula options, such as goat milk, which is what we had to use for my son. Ultimately, these are just my recommendations; choose what feels best for your little one.

Education

Your body is a miracle crafted by nature, just like the baby developing in your womb. I urge you to take time to recognize the transformations your body experiences, along with your baby, during pregnancy. A few things I found fascinating: By the end of the first trimester, 25% of your cardiac output, the volume of blood your heart pumps, is directed to the uterus to nourish your baby while you continue to receive your essential nutrients. Also, your ribcage instinctively expands by up to 2 inches to accommodate your growing baby.

Exploring your baby's growth enhances the awe of your little miracle. By eight weeks into gestation, your baby's main organs begin to develop, and by week 13, which signals the start of the second trimester, these organs are fully matured and will continue to grow throughout the pregnancy. Additionally, the placenta, which is a temporary organ that forms during pregnancy to house your baby and provide them nutrients through the umbilical cord, expands three times its original size during this time.

Every woman's body is unique, so comprehending the various birthing signals and processes is valuable. For instance, only 1 in 10 mothers have their water break before labor begins. This emphasizes the importance of being in tune with your body and recognizing potential signs of labor. Nausea and vomiting can occur during labor and childbirth, along with diarrhea, so it's wise to carry items for these reactions in your car while you're on your way to the birthing facility. Additionally, the surge of oxytocin after delivery might cause shaking or shivering, mimicking the sensation of being cold, even when you aren't.

Understanding post-birth information about you and your baby can also be beneficial. What should you anticipate regarding postpartum bleeding, and when is it necessary to seek further medical assistance? Are there any lifting restrictions based on your type of delivery? Within the first three days, your baby's stomach triples in size, coinciding with your milk supply, and your baby's first bowel movement typically occurs 24-48 hours after birth. This initial stool is tarry and known as 'meconium,' lasting a few days. While changing your baby's diaper, there may be a substance that appears to be blood, but this is referred to as 'brick dust,' which indicates your baby is dehydrated. Babies usually begin producing tears around three weeks after birth, once their tear ducts have fully developed.

A lot of my pregnancy and birth education came from my prenatal yoga teacher certification and my doula. If a doula is not local to you or it is not within your budget, many provide helpful information via blogs. Apps are also available to help you track the progress of your baby, which can be fun to follow. You can also ask your birthing facility about local classes being offered. The additional upside of attending these classes is that they allow you to connect with other expectant mothers, which adds another level of emotional support throughout the process, and you certainly can't have enough of that.

Post-Birth

After your baby is born, there are several key decisions to make. The first one is whether to delay clamping the umbilical cord. I strongly recommend researching this topic, as delaying the clamping has been associated with numerous health benefits. Some of these benefits include improved brain development, increased red blood cell volume, which transports oxygen from the lungs throughout the body, and a boost in iron intake, which is vital for your baby's growth and development.

You'll also need to decide if you'd like them to administer erythromycin, an eye medicine for your baby. It's not mandatory; you can choose to decline it. As always, consult with your healthcare provider about what's best for your baby and trust your instincts.

Another choice is deciding if you want to vaccinate your baby. This subject can feel daunting. During my pregnancy, I conducted thorough research to make educated decisions for my son. "The Vaccine Book" by Robert W. Sears, MD was a particularly helpful resource that provided unbiased information.

The Golden Hour

Regardless of how you welcomed your child into the world, the 'Golden Hour' offers significant advantages for both parents and your baby. Research demonstrates the benefits of skin-to-skin contact right after birth and its lasting emotional and physiological effects.

After almost 10 months of growing inside you, your baby is now facing the outside world for the first time, which can be overwhelming for them. They became accustomed to your heartbeat, finding comfort in it while in the womb. Once born, lying on your chest allows them to hear your heartbeat again, and your gentle touch can help calm them, significantly reducing their cries as you nurture their emotional needs.

Not only are you catering to their emotional needs, but their physical as well. When your baby is born, it cannot control its body temperature independently. By cuddling against you, the warmth from your body helps your baby maintain an average body temperature.

If you are a parent whose baby requires NICU care, prioritizing skin-to-skin contact can help stabilize your baby's blood pressure, heart rate, and respiratory rate while enhancing oxygen saturation levels, the percentage of oxygen in your baby's red blood cells. This practice also triggers the release of oxytocin, often referred to as the bonding hormone, strengthening the connection between you and your baby. Additionally, oxytocin plays a role in mood regulation and may assist in alleviating postpartum depression.

The bond created during the Golden Hour encourages the baby to latch and instinctively start suckling, initiating breastfeeding. Due to this initiation, the baby tends to feed for longer durations.

The 'Golden Hour' is such a magical time with your baby. You participated in your Olympic event of birth, and you've brought your baby into the world. You've won the gold. Cherish it.

Birth Emotional Imprints

It wasn't until I became pregnant that I recognized how many women carry emotional scars from their births. Although I won't recount the heartbreaking stories I've heard, I extend my deepest sympathies if your experience was painful. For such a pivotal event in your life, these memories are not what you hoped for.

If your birth required intervention, and depending on the scenario and its severity, I suggest focusing on not only the physical health of you and your baby but also the energetic and emotional health. If a situation occurred that left an emotional imprint on you, your baby, and others involved, you can turn to measures such as Reiki and other modalities to assist in clearing the residue of energies from this imprint. As you learned in the emotional body chapter, the emotions associated with an impactful imprint must be released. If not, over time they can cause harm to the physical body.

I understand the birth you envisioned was taken from you, but you can claim your power back. These memories won't be erased, but the energies and emotions associated with these memories will unchain them from you, giving you the freedom you deserve to live your life healthfully and happily.

CHAPTER 14

The 4th Trimester

As we drove away with the birthing center in our rearview mirror, now a new family of three, we joked that renting a car was more challenging than bringing home our son. As first-time parents, we were completely unsure of what to do: struggling with diaper changes, downloading apps to monitor his feeding schedule, and trying to understand what he was signaling with his cries. When we thought we had mastered the art of keeping our little one alive and settling into a routine, everything would change, and we'd have to start the process all over again.

Alongside the task of nurturing a tiny human, postpartum brings its own set of unique challenges. While others can describe their postpartum experiences, nothing truly prepares you for this new chapter of motherhood. You have to live it, breathe it, and experience it for yourself.

At times, I felt so lonely despite never being alone. My son slept beside me and was attached to me when he ate and when I ate, and even in most bathroom visits and showers, I had him in his bassinet on the floor near me. I recall one memory when I was alone with my son when he was only a few weeks old. I was so tired, and all I wanted that day was a shower. In the hopes of giving myself what

I so desperately wanted and needed, I spent almost an hour and a half rocking, cuddling, and consoling him, but all he wanted was to be in my arms.

As much as I loved our bonding time, a shower was the only thing on my mind. I finally put him down in the bassinet and hopped in the shower, leaving the door open so I could see him, and he could see me. In less than 30 seconds, he was wailing. I watched him cry as I quickly rinsed the soap from my body, which I had hurriedly applied. It would be another day of not washing my hair, but at least my body was clean—well, cleaner than before. I stepped out of the shower, quickly toweled off, and got dressed. The entire event was under five minutes, but the way his helpless cries penetrated my heart is still there today. The irony of this memory is that when I did receive help during my postpartum period and could take a long shower, all I really wanted was to hold my son.

As I tried to keep all the plates spinning, I was surviving on just a few hours of sleep each night, awkwardly dealing with my fluctuating hormones, sometimes crying without clear reasons. While I valued my friends' efforts to visit or get together, I often preferred solitude. This led me to question myself, wondering if I was doing enough during my postpartum period or falling short. Should I be socializing more or less?

I longed to regain my independence, as I had to rely on others while I healed from giving birth. Requesting assistance was a fundamental realization I had to confront. At times, I resented the help I received, wishing to care for my son on my terms, free from outside opinions. Then I reminded myself how fortunate I was to have support when many mothers didn't have that privilege; I often criticized myself for my feelings, which only imposed more self-judgment.

I recall my frustration during the overwhelming newness and fatigue when my mom friends would say, "Hang in there. It gets easier, I promise." Some days, I thought I'd never see the light at the end of the tunnel. Each day felt like a repeat of the last, as the day blended into the night and night into the day. I remember telling my husband I wanted to feel 'normal' again. This led me into a grieving process, as I realized that what I once considered 'normal' would never be again. While I knew things would change, I had no idea how different they would truly be until I experienced it myself.

The awareness of what my new 'normal' looked like led me down a path of sorting through my loss of identity. I questioned if all the hard work and dedication I put into my Reiki practice would still be who I wanted to be. Could I still show up as the wife I aspired to be? Would I make my son proud to call me his mother? I didn't want to let anyone down, especially myself.

Three months into postpartum, I emerged from a fog I didn't realize I was in, which left me feeling like an impostor. Here I was, writing this book on energy and mindfulness, yet I wasn't fully embodying these tools the way I once did. For years, my peers had relied on me as their backbone for support, yet I couldn't even support myself. This is when I had an epiphany.

For the first time since I had given birth, I gave myself grace for what I was feeling instead of shaming myself or passing judgment for it. Postpartum was humbling me in new, necessary ways to help me evolve into the woman and mother I am today. This moment was the revelation I needed to be the turning point in my postpartum journey. I then realized this was the stage of me losing myself, only to rediscover a new part of me I never knew existed. I'd never felt so lost yet incredibly satisfied and fulfilled. The oxymoron hit hard.

Leaning on Reiki and other modalities became essential in my postpartum recovery. When I felt lost, I realized it was quite the opposite. These modalities were gifts to bring awareness to my present. I felt raw and real emotions as I experienced motherhood for the first time and settled into the new skin I now wore. I began to embrace the mess of motherhood instead of resisting the changes I was encountering.

Motherhood is the unspoken bond between women, tethering us in unity, and as a mom, you wear the title as a badge of honor, but that badge doesn't come without its struggles. I know the hard days are complex, and it's okay to feel whatever emotions you're feeling. Remember, this is just a chapter in time, but you don't remain here. Give your mind and body grace, be gentle with yourself, and trust your intuition on what's best for you and your baby during your postpartum.

It was six months into my 4th trimester before I really felt like I was ready to socialize and felt creative enough to fully pick back up writing this book. It's not how I envisioned my journey into motherhood, but it's how my story was meant to unfold.

Studies show it takes up to two full years for a mother's hormones to stabilize after birth. I do believe the holistic remedies shared later in this chapter can help shorten this time frame, but if they don't, that is absolutely okay. Take all the time you need to heal.

If you are a mama who feels you're struggling with postpartum depression, please reach out to someone for support.

Be Present

Birthing my son forced me to slow down physically and energetically. As my body was physically recovering for months after giving birth, the inevitable stillness of that period made me re-evaluate my otherwise contented life. This is the deeper lesson our children provide us during this time. Having a baby is the Universe giving you permission to slow down, be present, and witness the gifts around you.

Even though there were times when I was breastfeeding, I felt more like a cow than a woman and mother, I stayed as present as possible during the feedings. I reminded myself I would never get that feeding, that moment, back. Each feeding became another opportunity to have an emotional involvement with my son that would build upon the foundation of our exclusive bond. Fulfilling not just his nutritional needs but also his emotional ones, showing him my dedication to nurturing him however and whenever he needed. The way he would look up at me proved he understood my sincerity and conviction as we gained mutual trust for one another. Instead of these feedings feeling like a chore, these thoughts shifted my perspective to the intentional meaning of what we were creating together.

As your child develops daily, you take in these little milestones, a reminder of the beauty in the present. Watching your baby find their toes for the first time, hearing them giggle, and seeing their first tooth finally pop through after the restless days and nights of teething are gifts granted for living in the present moment. Watching how my son would marvel at a new toy, intensely focused and processing how the toy felt in his hand, how he would twitch his wrist so he could see the toy from all angles, reminded me how we need more time to slow down and soak in the things around us. There is always so much to be grateful for and to admire. We must choose to see it.

Your Tribe

As each day passed, I became more confident in my new role as I leaned on my tribe of people around me. I reached out to friends who were already mamas, which was super helpful during this period. Asking them questions, sometimes crying on the phone, and telling them how overwhelmed I felt when my son would nurse for over 5 hours a day (more on this next) and how I struggled to feel accomplished at the end of the day because I was used to being a mega productive person. These calls would shift my energy and mindset, and I would realize that I was being productive. I was keeping a human alive and being an integral part of his development. That was a full-time position that required overtime and not a job to take lightly.

Just as you found your tribe during pregnancy, having the right support around you during postpartum is necessary. You may also find your tribe differs during this phase of life, and that's okay, too. Being around other like-minded mamas will provide emotional and mental support during this time. If you're finding it hard to find other mamas to connect with, I highly encourage joining a community of some sort, whether that be online or locally. It's our duty to care for each other.

Lactation

Every mama I've ever spoken to has struggled with lactation in some capacity. Whether they struggled to get their baby to latch or had a low or abundant milk supply, all have posed their challenges. I desperately wanted to breastfeed and convinced my husband to buy a massive deep freezer for our garage where I planned to store my Magic Mama Meals and my excess supply of breastmilk. I entered this phase of motherhood blindly and didn't give it much thought until my son was ten weeks old, and I noticed a significant shift in his mood. He would wake up as his typical happy-go-lucky self, but by 3 or 4 pm, our world would turn upside down into a non-stop crying fest. Nothing seemed to soothe him.

After a few days of attentive observation, I felt like his latch wasn't as strong, and my intuition told me he was hungry, which was why he was crying. While breastfeeding, he still seemed to feed long enough, but if he genuinely wasn't latching well, I thought maybe this was the reason behind his afternoon tears.

My husband was in Malaysia during this time, and we spoke briefly only once daily. When I told him I thought our son wasn't latching well now, he was confused, just as I was, and rightfully so. Why all of a sudden? He seemed to be gaining weight, eating frequently and for a long enough duration. Despite my confusion and lack of complete understanding, I listened to my gut.

The next day, I was finally venturing out into the world for some self-care and had my first pelvic floor therapy session to help heal my diastasis recti, a condition caused by the separation of my abdominal muscles during pregnancy. I planned the appointment for 11 am, which aligned nicely with my son's nap schedule, similar to other appointments I had in recent weeks. I breastfed him right before we left, packed everything up, and he napped on the ride down, everything went according to plan. However, he woke up and became fussy once we arrived, which was out of character, especially this early in the day.

During my session, the pelvic floor therapist held my son and worked on soothing him while instructing me on therapy postures to strengthen my pelvic floor. Luckily, with my yoga and Pilates background, her cues were all the direction I needed.

On my way out, I, only half-jokingly, asked if she needed me to pay her for babysitting during my session or if that was included. "What a disaster that was." I thought to myself as I felt defeated while shutting my car door to feed my son again in the backseat. That was my final straw. As I was breastfeeding my son, I called the birthing center and spoke to the lactation specialist I had seen right after giving birth.

When speaking with her, I explained what we had been experiencing. During our conversation, she informed me that at about six to eight weeks, the mama's body goes from the "we just birthed a baby" to "now we have to keep them alive state," and your production starts to regulate. Timeline-wise, this lined up exactly when my son became super fussy in the afternoons. My production must have just started to regulate, and when he had to work for the milk on his own, he wasn't getting enough.

The next day, we had our appointment with the lactation specialist. Once settling in, we recapped our conversation from the day prior. She then suggested we give my son a fresh diaper, weigh him, feed him, and then weigh him again to see how much he consumed during the feeding. As she placed him on the scale before we began our feeding experiment, she said, "11 pounds, 6 ounces." "Oh wow! That seems good!" I exclaimed. The look on her face told me otherwise. "He's about a pound underweight for his age." She said grimly. "What?" My face in shock, I continued. "We were just at the pediatrician about two weeks ago, and there was no mention of him being underweight."

I then latched my son on the right breast and began feeding him. The lactation specialist immediately said, "Oh yeah, that's certainly not an impressive latch." Feeling discouraged yet hopeful for a resolution, I continued to feed him for about 15 minutes. We then weighed him. In 15 minutes of feeding, he only took in 1.5 ounces. I then latched him on the left side, let him feed for almost 10 minutes, and weighed him again. The scale showed he only took in another .5 ounces, showing that in nearly 25 minutes of feeding, he'd only consumed 2 ounces of breastmilk, cutting him short an ounce or two of what he needed.

"That's a lot of hard work for such a little guy," she said as she reached her gloved hand into his mouth to feel his palate. "He has a high-arched palate too, almost like he has a cleft palate, which he doesn't, right?" "No. It was confirmed at our 18-week anatomy scan he didn't have one." I said. "Ok, has he been taking bottles, or have you introduced them?" She asked. "The few we've given, he's taken just fine but hasn't fully finished them," I responded.

As we looked back at the notes in our file from our 24-hour post-birth appointment, she noted that my son's jaw was a little retracted at birth. This was likely due to him not closing his mouth in utero, which, as we recently learned about his arched palate, was also a possible culprit. When his mouth was continually resting open in utero, his tongue didn't flatten his palate.

She then explained how the shape of his palate would make it challenging to take a standard nipple on a bottle. Hoping it would help, she provided a special feeding bottle for children with cleft palates.

"You were right, mama." She said to me in a soft, supportive voice. My eyes began to fill with tears. "He wasn't getting enough to eat, and by the afternoon, he was so hungry and inconsolable." The tears that once filled my eyes now trickled down my face. "Thank you for taking the time to listen to me. With everything we've been through the past few weeks, I wondered if I was going crazy."

The lactation specialist not only encouraged me, but I also felt seen, heard, and validated. Yes, I was a new mom, but my intuition had proven right again, and I felt empowered. I was ready to act on the necessary steps to get my son's weight up and make him feel full and happy again.

I committed to triple-feed him. For every feed, I would put him on the breast for 10-15 minutes, pump for 15-20 minutes, and then feed him the 3-4 ounces I pumped. This also had to be done every few hours to keep my production up. We scoured Amazon for another bottle that worked better for the shape of his mouth to help him feed and began seeing a craniosacral therapist. Craniosacral therapy is an alternative treatment that uses gentle touch to manipulate the cranium or skull, and this would help appropriately align his retracted jaw.

After a week of dedicated triple feeding, he had gained nearly a pound and was back to his usual cheerful self. As he continued to grow, his daily milk consumption averaged 30 ounces, 6 more than the average baby, yet I could only produce about 22 ounces. To bridge the gap, I had to include baby formula as a bottle or two to make up the deficit. I knew in my mind, 'fed was best,' but I felt like my body was letting me down, but more importantly, I felt like I was letting my son down. Then, remembering the power of my mind, I shifted my perspective and expressed gratitude for all my body had accomplished up to that point and the hurdles I'd overcome. I had so much to be proud of: my tenacity to listen to my intuition when others doubted me and the dedication I made to feed my son. This mindset helped bring me peace with the idea of using baby formula to supplement his feedings when I wasn't producing enough breastmilk.

After two dedicated months of triple feeding, our son continued to thrive and was in the high percentile of growth in weight and height, and the craniosacral therapy work corrected his retracted jaw.

I desperately wanted to breastfeed for a year, but once my son started getting his teeth in at 5.5 months, my supply started to dry up. I know many mamas who have driven themselves crazy, putting so much pressure on themselves to 'perform' for their babies. Your baby doesn't care how they are fed; they care about how you show up and nurture them. Strive not to rob yourself of this precious time of motherhood. Sometimes, you may feel like a milking machine, but you're incredible! It's an intimate connection that only you can have with your baby as you feed and nourish them. Remember, you're not a failure if breastfeeding doesn't work out for you; be proud of your efforts. Lean on your tribe to support you through your lactation journey, whatever that looks like for you and your baby.

Holistic Mothering

There are many ways to support you and your baby holistically during your postpartum period. The modalities I'm sharing are ones I personally used and advocate for.

Chiropractic Care. Many people find the idea of visiting a chiropractor intimidating. Choosing a practitioner who makes you feel comfortable and whom you can trust with your care and that of your baby is vital. During my prenatal care, I saw my chiropractor regularly to ensure my pelvis remained aligned for delivery. I also committed to ongoing care for both me and my son after birth. I experienced a tear in the ligaments around my ribs during childbirth, which made it challenging to hold my son while standing; the adjustments significantly aided my healing process. I have two chiropractors I fully trust, each offering distinct styles of care. One follows a more traditional approach, while the other relies on intuition to guide his treatment, along with what you've expressed needs attention. I've also trained him in Reiki I, so those sessions are blended with healing work, which I appreciate. He integrates many modalities into his sessions, myofascial release being one of my favorites.

Fascia is a thin connective tissue located beneath the skin that encases and supports every organ, blood vessel, nerve, bone, and muscle. (Interestingly, fascia can also store emotions, similar to other body parts. If your fascia tends to remain tight or struggles to release, consider examining any emotions you might be holding onto and find ways to process and release them.) When fascia is taut, it can result in immobility and discomfort. Tension of the fascia can pull on bones, therefore, leading to misalignments. In myofascial release, practitioners apply gentle pressure using their hands or tools, like a massage gun, to ease this connective tissue. Once the fascia is relaxed, chiropractic adjustments can be performed more easily, enabling everything to align properly.

My son received his first chiropractic adjustment when he was four days old. I believe that keeping his body in alignment has significantly supported his development. Whenever he showed signs of constipation, an adjustment generally resolved the issue. The only exception was during a major growth spurt. When a child goes through a large growth phase, their body absorbs all the nutrients necessary for development, resulting in minimal waste to eliminate. This temporary decrease in elimination typically resolves within a few days.

We have continued his chiropractic care every two to three weeks, give or take, and I genuinely believe it has been crucial in him sleeping 11-13 hours each night and being an overall cheerful baby. Feeling unwell can make anyone irritable, including babies, who express discomfort primarily through crying. Birth is challenging for both you and your baby, so in my opinion, leaning on chiropractic care can not only help your recovery process but can maintain proper alignment of your baby's body to support their proper development. Additionally, I want to emphasize that adjustments for your little one involves minimal physical manipulation. They are quite subtle and often performed with a tool called an activator, which delivers quick, low-force adjustments to specific points, making them very precise. If your baby seems uncomfortable or distressed, I would always start with chiropractic care.

Reiki is a holistic approach beneficial for both you and your baby, particularly following a difficult birth or one that caused emotional scarring. Administering Reiki to yourself and your baby or working with a qualified practitioner can assist in releasing emotional imprints. In doing so may reduce the long-term adverse effects that these emotions could have on your physical well-being. Reiki can help clear any generational energies passed down to your child, even after an uneventful birth. I strongly recommend regular Reiki sessions to aid your recovery, assist with pain management, promote better sleep when possible, and support hormonal balance.

Additionally, Reiki creates a sense of safety and comfort for your baby while they transition to life outside your womb. If you've chosen to adopt, giving your baby Reiki can enhance your baby's sense of security. On a physical level, Reiki supports the endocrine system, which is crucial for growth, specifically the thyroid, as the hormones it produces are essential for your child's brain development.

In summary, Reiki is a superb option for maintaining both your bodies in a parasympathetic (rest and digest) state, which is important for optimal health. Feel free to reference chapters two and three on Reiki, and its benefits.

Acupuncture, like Reiki, helps balance your body's Qi, pronounced "chi" (energy). While Reiki treats the whole body, acupuncturists use needles on specific acupuncture points. These points lie along the body's meridians, which I call "energy highways." Each meridian is linked to specific organs, and as noted in the chapter "Reiki and the Physical Body," disruptions in energy can cause imbalances, which in Chinese Medicine impair organ function. After giving birth, your overall chi diminishes, particularly affecting the energy of your spleen, liver, and kidneys. The spleen is responsible for producing blood and chi and digesting food. This is why your Magic Mama Meals should focus on warm, nourishing foods that help restore your spleen energy. You want to avoid putting extra strain on your already depleted spleen by consuming cool foods. In Chinese Medicine, hair loss is frequently associated with kidney health, which is why many women notice increased hair loss during the postpartum period. If Reiki doesn't resonate with you, I strongly recommend trying acupuncture. It is a modality that has done wonders for me.

I explained how my intuition guided me to explore Kinesiology (Muscle Testing) for diagnosing my son's food sensitivities. Muscle testing is an effective alternative medicine method grounded in Sir Isaac Newton's Law of Motion, which states, "For every action in nature, there is an equal and opposite reaction," meaning that muscle weakness is induced by any internal disruptions your body is experiencing. I frequently rely on this approach for additional support for myself and my family and have had great success. If you find yourself in a situation where you are seeking answers but are uncertain about where to begin, I strongly recommend locating a credible practitioner near you.

Organic, cold pressed Coconut Oil is a staple I keep in my house to cook with, but it is also a go-to for many holistic uses. When my son was a newborn getting used to life outside the womb and having to wear a diaper, I used coconut oil for his diaper rash. I would use a popsicle stick or something similar to scoop a little dabble of the oil out and gently rub it over the rash. I did the same thing over the summer when there was a little more irritation from his sweat and the heat and friction from the diaper. Consistent use of the coconut oil for a few days cleared it up every time

I also used coconut oil to help eliminate his cradle cap. About two to three nights a week, 15 or so minutes before his bath, I would apply it on his scalp until it became a clear liquid and let it set. Then, while I had him in the bathtub, I'd use a gentle cradle cap brush in a circular motion to remove the flakes. It wasn't long before the cradle cap was gone.

When my son began teething, I used coconut oil to soothe the chapping on his sweet little face. I applied it throughout the day and used it to massage him, which is great for bonding. I've also used it when he has accidentally scratched his face while sleeping, and the scratch is gone after a few applications.

Coconut oil also came to the rescue for me when I was triple-feeding. After a few weeks, my nipples started to feel raw from pumping and feeding so much. I eventually applied a little coconut oil to my nipples to help lubricate them while pumping. This helped tremendously. I've also heard of moms using it for cracked and sore nipples.

I have crystals sprinkled throughout our home; selenite safeguards the energy of our space and purifies any energies that need to be discarded. I also have tourmaline under our mattress and couch to assist in keeping our energy grounded and shungite around our electronics and the baby camera in my son's room as it shields against EMF radiation. I also have my son wear a raw amber necklace that has helped reduce his teething pain and absorbs any negative energy he encounters.

In your 4th trimester, remember grace is your best friend. As your body is healing, take time to power down your mind. Rest is productive; remain as present as possible and lean on your tribe for help. You're doing an amazing job, and I'm proud of you. You've got this, mama.

CHAPTER 15

Raising an Energetically Aware Child

As a child, I frequently fell ill. As the usual vomiting induced, my mom would take me to the doctor. They would typically conclude that I had caught some stomach bug from school or daycare. Suppositories were prescribed and given to me, as they were the only remedy that would eventually stop my vomiting.

This experience persisted throughout my childhood, leaving a lasting memory. Now that my mother understands my empathic nature and sensitivity to energy, she believes, as I do, that my uncontrollable vomiting was a result of the stress in our home. Despite not knowing what energy was back then, I was subconsciously absorbing the energies around me. Much like a five-gallon bucket, my small body would eventually fill with these low vibrational, toxic energies until it overflowed. I believe that vomiting was my body's only means of purging this unwanted energy.

Little did I know that experiencing such sensitivity as a child would help me relate to children over 20 years later in my Reiki practice.

During my time in the 'healing hallway,' where I saw Reiki clients, I met another practitioner with three children. Her youngest, an eight-year-old, had begun experiencing debilitating migraines that kept her from attending school. She could only find relief in a darkened room, as light amplified her discomfort. After weeks of persistent migraines and missed school days, the practitioner decided to consult a neurologist, who recommended an MRI to investigate the situation further.

The MRI revealed that her brain appeared healthy and normal, with no concerning issues identified. The mother, confused, witnessed her daughter's severe pain up close. Feeling helpless and at a loss, she decided to reach out to me for a Reiki session.

"My intuition told me you're who I needed her to see." She told me as we started the distant Reiki session over Zoom. With her daughter curled up beside her, I could see her daughter's discomfort. I explained to her and her daughter how I would conduct the session and what they may expect.

When I started the Reiki session, my intuition and the energy I sensed immediately revealed the issue. This sweet young girl was absorbing the energies of those around her, much like I did at her age. I began asking her questions, though she was initially quite shy. With her mother's presence for comfort, she felt more at ease to respond to my questions. Her responses validated what I was detecting energetically. In addition to carrying other's energies, she was also experiencing significant pressure from her father regarding her performance in soccer. She didn't want to disappoint him, which contributed to the stress her little body was already harboring.

While providing Reiki to her daughter during the session, I emphasized to both of them the importance of safeguarding their energy, particularly the daughter's. I explained to them how to cleanse their personal energy and the energy in their home, exactly as the guidance given in the 'Energetic Responsibility' chapter.

About an hour later, when we concluded the session, I informed them what to expect: the daughter might feel very tired or experience a sudden burst of energy now that her energy wasn't congested and flowing through her body. Based on what I sensed during the session, I strongly believed the daughter would be extremely fatigued since her autonomic nervous system had shifted from fight or flight to rest and digest.

The following day, when I checked in with the mother, she shared that after the session, as she was putting her daughter to bed, her daughter asked, "Mommy, how did Mel know all that about me when she doesn't even *know* me?" The mother replied, "Because that's what Mel does, honey, and it helps people feel better." Her daughter slept soundly through the night and woke up the next morning migraine-free.

Months after our session, the mother reached out to express her gratitude and provide an update. They began a daily circle of prayer for her daughter before school and made efforts to regularly cleanse her energy. She also discussed the session with her husband, addressing the pressure their daughter felt to excel in soccer and the fear of disappointing him, which was causing her significant unconscious stress. They shifted their focus on soccer from intense competition to play, which not only alleviated her daughter's stress but also improved her performance. The mother concluded her message by noting that her daughter hadn't experienced a migraine since our session. She wrapped up the call, saying, "I don't know exactly how Reiki works, but all I know is it works."

This session also taught me a valuable lesson, especially as I had just become a mother myself. Not only was this little girl sensitive to energy, but she was also feeling overwhelmed by the added stress of competition, which was making her energy bucket overflow. It made me realize that just like adults, children can bear different amounts of stress, some can handle a saucer, others a plate or a platter. It's our duty as consciously aware mothers to support them according to their needs, rather than our assumptions. While some children thrive in competitive sports, others may not find joy in it, and that is perfectly okay. Our goal should be to listen and observe our children for who they truly are and who they are meant to be so they can remain as energetically aligned as possible.

As I mentioned in the Reiki and Children section of the 'Why Reiki' chapter, I often encountered children suffering from unexplained ailments. I can confidently say that for every child and teenager I worked with, once we focused on clearing their energy bodies and they consistently applied the tools to safeguard and cleanse their energy, their ailments disappeared. These transformations didn't always occur immediately; in many cases, the transformation took several months, sometimes almost a year, but every one of them saw positive results. Consistency was key.

If you find yourself in a position where your child is experiencing unexplainable or unidentified ailments, or your motherly intuition tells you something just feels "off," trust that feeling. I encourage you to reference this book to investigate whether your child is suffering from energetic imbalances or their energy body bucket is overflowing, similar to the stories shared above. Even if other measures are required to remedy what your child is experiencing, supporting their energy body will only complement those efforts.

The Power of Words

As discussed in this book, everything is energy. This includes the words you say to yourself and your child, each word casting its own frequency.

In the 'Mindful Mama' chapter, research illustrates how negative words distort water droplets while positive words create stunning snowflake patterns, each uniquely formed by positivity. Given the power of frequency in our words, it's crucial to speak kindly to yourself. Your words impact not just your own mindset but also reverberate throughout your body. When you consistently use kind language with yourself, you cultivate a habit that enables you to respond positively to your surroundings and to others, especially your child. You are actively or passively shaping their belief systems regarding communication with themselves, others, and the world around them. Words are powerful and important, so choose them wisely.

I strongly recommend integrating positive and intentional affirmations with your child to foster positive self-talk and reinforcement. As mentioned in the 'Baby Communication' chapter, this can begin while your baby is still in utero, as their hearing is fully developed by around six months. Additionally, it's crucial to encourage your child, offering praise to enhance their confidence, sharing the qualities you appreciate in them, and assuring them of your unwavering support. This approach will help them feel secure, cherished, and self-assured in their endeavors.

I think teaching your child these positive affirmations are essential to incorporate when your child is attending school. The saying we've all heard, "Sticks and stones may break my bones, but words will never hurt me," is cute but certainly a false statement. The truth is, negative words do hurt, and they stick with us. In a world where bullying is at its highest, I think it's important now more than ever to teach our children the power of words and how, when they say hurtful things, they can have significant ramifications on a peer. The other side of that is how speaking positively to their peers has a brilliant effect on not only your child's well-being but also the well-being of those they are speaking to. It's never too early to teach your child kindness; the world as a whole needs more of it.

Along with teaching your child to speak kindly to themselves and others, also instill the importance of gratitude. Expressing gratitude releases dopamine and serotonin, the two neurotransmitters responsible for their emotions. These chemicals not only make them feel good, but can also improve their sleep, mood, and immunity. I call this a mom win, for sure.

When focusing on language, consider the inevitable mistakes your child will make. Be mindful of your words and choose them carefully. They are likely already upset with themselves for their slipup. When your child makes a mistake, reassure them that it's okay to make errors, as this is part of the learning process.

This also applies to you when you make a mistake in their presence. Your child observes how to feel about various situations through your responses, including how you manage your errors. You are teaching them how to react and engage with themselves when they face their own mistakes, so be the appropriate role model for your child.

For example, let's say while making breakfast, you accidentally spill milk while pouring it into your child's cup. You react by grimacing and reprimanding yourself with derogatory words such as, "Gosh, I'm so stupid. I should have been paying attention." This reaction shows your child that when they make a mistake, they are stupid, which is so untrue. Not to mention, they will pick up on the language you used to speak to yourself when you made the mistake and respond to themselves in the same manner. When you make a mistake, make a conscious effort to handle the situation how you'd want your child to respond to themselves when they make mistakes.

Another example is you have made a mistake at work, and your boss is upset with you. You're also very disappointed with yourself that you made the error. You come home with body language that clearly shows you're angry and upset. Your child can feel the energy you are exuding and asks you what's wrong. You automatically reply, "Nothing. I'm fine," in a short, snarky tone.

In this scenario, I think it's important to communicate your feelings to your child, sharing what's appropriate and expressing that you're disappointed in yourself for making a mistake. You feel like you not only let yourself down, but your boss and team at work down. This openness helps your child learn to identify their own emotions and the energy associated with these emotions. This, in turn, gives them a sturdier emotional landscape as they mature, teaching them to acknowledge, express, and navigate their feelings instead of suppressing them and causing potential issues later on. There is power in vulnerability, especially with our children.

Mindfulness

Everything shared in the 'Mindful Mama' chapter is applicable to your child. Being their guide for these practices will help them excel.

Along with having them incorporate positive and intentional affirmations, teach them the power of mental rehearsal and that they have the magic within them to create their reality. As an interactive family activity, make an intentional power board for the family to post on the refrigerator or to frame and put on the mantle. Choose purposeful photos that express gratitude and/or the family vacation you all want to enjoy together that year. Encourage your child to make their own power board so they can see their own dreams and aspirations come to fruition.

Incorporate breathwork into your routine, particularly when your child is stressed. Research indicates that children who engage in mindfulness practices, like breathwork, experience fewer temper tantrums. If tantrums occur, stay calm and present while reminding them to breathe. Be aware that your emotions can influence them; if you're tense, they may mirror that tension, exacerbating the situation. Encourage your child to practice the Ujjayi breath, also known as ocean breathing. This involves inhaling through the nose with the mouth closed, creating space at the back of the throat while taking deep belly breaths to expand the diaphragm. They should keep their mouth closed, and their jaw relaxed while exhaling through the nose, maintaining that space at the back of the throat. As they exhale, their breath should become audible, mimicking the sound of ocean waves. They can continue this practice until they feel calmer. Remember, the Ujjayi breath activates the Vagus Nerve, a key component of the parasympathetic nervous system that helps return the body to a state of rest and digestion, therefore reducing stress. To watch an instructional video on how to perform the Ujjay breath, visit www.melbraun.com.

You can also use breathwork to teach your child how to meditate, have them repeat their favorite positive affirmations, or give them a visualization such as scanning their body. Regular meditation with your child can help them sleep better, learn to self-regulate, improve their focus, mood, and creativity, and help them manage stress. For an extra bonus, meditate as a bonding activity with your child, and maybe get the whole family involved.

Teaching your child the importance of journaling can start early. It allows them to step away from screens and reconnect with themselves. Writing can create a safe environment for them to express their feelings, which can lower stress and anxiety, helping them let go of pent-up emotions instead of keeping them bottled up. Through journaling, they can develop greater self-awareness, enabling them to build a more confident self and explore their creativity. It's also a means for your child to declutter their thoughts, fostering their ability to be more present with you and those around them.

Encourage them to write down their hopes and dreams and who they aspire to be. Add this with their mental rehearsal, intentional affirmations, and their power board; now that's a powerful combination of mindfulness.

I believe our souls select our parents for a purpose: to learn essential lessons in this lifetime or to help us navigate challenges for our spiritual growth. This notion can be hard to accept, especially based on your upbringing. It's crucial to learn and evolve from these childhood experiences, as they fundamentally shaped who you are today. If your childhood doesn't align with your adult desires, consider examining your parents and their backgrounds. In my personal journey and my working with clients through Reiki, I've observed that parents do their best at that moment. If they caused you pain, it was likely rooted in their own unresolved and unhealed pain that they likely weren't even consciously aware of. I am sorry if this was your childhood experience, and while I don't condone their actions or behavior, understanding their perspective can allow you to forgive, let go, and heal.

The principles outlined in this book, when applied, will empower you to heal your emotional scars and release the negative generational imprints that have been passed down. You've learned to safeguard your energy and create an effective positive mindset. When combined, these elements will help you become less reactive, more empathetic, and fully present with your child. They deserve the best version of you, and you have the ability to shape their narrative. With you leading by example, you are giving your child the emotional, energetic, and mental tools they need to thrive and reach their full potential.

I've noticed millennials (born between 1981-1996) have seemed to be the initial generation that began the shifts that needed to take place, and Generation Z (born between 1997-2012) has taken it a step further by erasing the idea that therapy is taboo and outwardly expressing the power of the healing it can bring and instilling mindfulness practices as a routine. It is believed that the children being born from these two generations, Generation Alpha, (born between 2010-2024) will likely have longer life expectancies, and I can't help but believe that a major contribution of this stems from the courage millennials and Gen Z have had to release the generational imprints that were being passed down, and consciously living a more intentional and energetically aligned lifestyle. Generation Alpha is the largest generation in history, which has given me even more faith that the work millennials and Gen Z have done will create an even larger ripple throughout humanity, and that is pure magic, mama.

FINAL THOUGHTS

I hope this book has inspired you, encouraged you, and empowered you. It takes courage to face adversities head-on and take charge of your mental, emotional, and energetic well-being. With the tools given throughout this book, if committed to, I have no doubt you and your child will live out your full potential and even exceed it.

May you live life with an open mind, an open heart, and surrender as you choose to blindly follow the crumbs that are left before you. Trusting a higher guiding force is arranging your next chess move in life and having faith that everything is happening for you the way it's intended to. You have the power to sprinkle your magical pixie dust on everything in life because you are the magic that creates your reality.

My question today remains: who is Aria that I heard speaking to me on that hot July day, who told me, "I'm ready when you are; the world needs me."?

Since her initial communication, she has seamlessly guided me through every stage: from conception to pregnancy, birth, and now the launch of this book. Maybe she remains my unborn child or is my guardian angel. Perhaps her sole purpose was to help me embrace motherhood, allowing me not only to give birth to my son but also to this book. She was right; the world truly needed her, as the messages amongst these pages are how collectively we show up as a better version of ourselves and for our children, making a positive difference in the world. Regardless of Aria's identity, I am eternally grateful for her guidance in this beautiful fairytale of life I live. She inspired me to pursue the nugget of clues left for me, and I believe she continues to do so as she still communicates with me frequently.

INDEX

Asking for Signs 190
Aura 62
Birth Plan 197
Body Talk 90
Boundaries 141
Breathwork 110, 199
Chakras 54
Cleansing Your Energy and Space
   Cleansing your Space 73
   Energetic Cords 71
   How to Cleanse Your Space 75
   Visualization 70
Crystals 77
Emotional Imprints 209
Epigenetics 95
Fetal Origin 162
Find Your Tribe 139
Forest Bathing 114
Gratitude 112
Grid Clearing 166
Grounding 115
Holistic Mothering 220
Hospital Bag 200
Incubation Period 136
Intentional Affirmations 106
Intentional Power Board 104, 131
Intuition 189
Intuitive Gifts 187
Journaling 112, 134, 191
Kenyoku 71
Lactation 215
Magic Mama Meals 157

Meditation 108, 193
Mental Rehearsal 102
Mindful Movement 113
Mindfulness 108, 232
Post-Birth 207
Reiki 42, 43, 49, 50, 116, 130, 226, 227
Reiki and Children 35
R.E.S.T 118
Rituals 97
Safeguarding Your Energy 67
   Circle of Prayer 67
   Energy Bubble 68
   Grounding Visualization or Meditation 68
Silence 115
The 10-Minute Rule 116
The Golden Hour 208
Ujjay Breath 194
Your Tribe 215